Eastern Europe 1945–1969:
From Stalinism to Stagnation

Pearson
Education

We work with leading authors to develop the
strongest educational materials in history,
bringing cutting-edge thinking and best learning
practice to a global market.

Under a range of well-known imprints, including
Longman, we craft high-quality print and electronic
publications which help readers to understand and
apply their content, whether studying or at work.

To find out more about the complete range of our
publishing please visit us on the World Wide Web at:
www.pearsoneduc.com

SEMINAR STUDIES IN HISTORY

# Eastern Europe 1945–1969:

## From Stalinism to Stagnation

BEN FOWKES

Longman

*An imprint of* **Pearson Education**

Harlow, England · London · New York · Reading, Massachusetts · San Francisco · Toronto · Don Mills, Ontario · Sydney
Tokyo · Singapore · Hong Kong · Seoul · Taipei · Cape Town · Madrid · Mexico City · Amsterdam · Munich · Paris · Milan

**Pearson Education Limited**
Edinburgh Gate
Harlow
Essex CM20 2JE
England
*and Associated Companies throughout the world.*

*Visit us on the World Wide Web at:*
www.pearsoned-ema.com

First published 2000

© Pearson Education Limited 2000

The right of Ben Fowkes to be identified as author
of this work has been asserted by him in accordance
with the Copyright, Designs and Patents Act 1988.

ISBN: 0-582-32693-1 PPR

**British Library Cataloguing-in-Publication Data**

A catalogue record for this book is
available from the British Library

**Library of Congress Cataloging-in-Publication Data**
Fowkes, Ben.
    Eastern Europe 1945–1969: from stalinism to stagnation / Frank Benjamin Michael Fowkes.
        p. cm. -- (Seminar studies in history)
    Includes bibliographical references and index.
    ISBN 0-582-32693-1 (ppr)
        1. Europe, Eastern--Politics and government--1945–1989. I. Title. II. Series.

DJK50 .F69 2000
320.947--dc21
                                                                99-089001

Set by 7 in 10/12 Sabon Roman
Printed in Malaysia, KVP

# CONTENTS

# INTRODUCTION TO THE SERIES

Such is the pace of historical enquiry in the modern world that there is an ever-widening gap between the specialist article or monograph, incorporating the results of current research, and general surveys, which inevitably become out of date. Seminar Studies in History are designed to bridge this gap. The series was founded by Patrick Richardson in 1966 and his aim was to cover major themes in British, European and World history. Between 1980 and 1996 Roger Lockyer continued his work, before handing the editorship over to Clive Emsley and Gordon Martel. Clive Emsley is Professor of History at the Open University, while Gordon Martel is Professor of International History at the University of Northern British Columbia, Canada and Senior Research Fellow at De Montfort University.

All the books are written by experts in their field who are not only familiar with the latest research but have often contributed to it. They are frequently revised, in order to take account of new information and interpretations. They provide a selection of documents to illustrate major themes and provoke discussion, and also a guide to further reading. The aim of *Seminar Studies* is to clarify complex issues without over-simplifying them, and to stimulate readers into deepening their knowledge and understanding of major themes and topics.

# NOTE ON REFERENCING SYSTEM

Readers should note that numbers in square brackets [5] refer them to the corresponding entry in the Bibliography at the end of the book (specific page numbers are given in italics). A number in square brackets preceded by *Doc.* [*Doc. 5*] refers readers to the corresponding item in the Documents section which follows the main text. Asterisks mark items listed in the Glossary.

# PREFACE

Eastern Europe is defined in this book as the part of Europe which came under communist rule after the Second World War. This definition is historical rather than geographical. It expresses the reality that over the whole of the area from the Baltic to the Adriatic, from the River Elbe to the Rhodope Mountains, the methods and objectives of communist rule, and the impact of communism on nations and societies, were practically identical. This fact served very quickly to mark off these countries as a whole from the West. This is why Greece is never, and Bulgaria always, regarded as part of Eastern Europe. Admittedly, the definition is fuzzy at the edges. East Germany ought perhaps to be excluded (it often has been by writers on this subject). Perhaps the Baltic countries of Estonia, Latvia and Lithuania deserve inclusion. But they were directly incorporated into the Soviet Union rather than being given the relative independence from which the rest of Eastern Europe benefited after 1945. Moreover, the story of the 'three that got away' – Finland, Austria and Greece – is possibly also relevant, as it throws light on communist techniques of achieving power and reasons for failure, as well as on Stalin's postwar strategic options.

Despite these hesitations, we shall concentrate here on the central bloc of satellite states, 'Europe of the Eight', namely East Germany (known officially after 1949 as the German Democratic Republic, before that as the Soviet Occupation Zone, or SBZ); Czechoslovakia; Poland; Hungary; Romania; Bulgaria; Yugoslavia; and Albania. These are the European countries that passed under communist control between 1944 and 1948 and remained in that situation for the next forty or so years. Differences in development and culture will also sometimes compel us to view Eastern Europe as composed of two parts, namely East Central and South Eastern Europe, divided by a line running to the east and south of Hungary. The topic, too, has been divided into two parts: before and after 1969. This book is the first part. It covers the seizure of power, the period of Stalinism and subsequent attempts at reform within the system. The period of decline after 1969 is dealt with in a companion volume by Dr Bülent Gökay.

# ACKNOWLEDGEMENTS

The publishers are grateful to the following for permission to use copyright material:

Photograph 1 'Sceptical East German workers listen to Fritz Selbmann, GDR Minister of Heavy Industry, opening a coke and lignite works, 31 August 1955' from *Anatomy of a Dictatorship: Inside the GDR 1949–1989*, pp. 148–9, Oxford University Press, permission sought from SED Bildarchiv, Berlin (Fulbrook, 1995)

Photograph 2 'Communists demonstrate in Belgrade promising the doubling of wheat production in 1947, dominated by Tito's picture' from *Yugoslavia as History*, p. 244, Cambridge University Press, used with permission from the Museum of the City of Belgrade (Lampe, 1996)

Photograph 3 'The female student militia on parade in Tirana, 1964' from *The Albanians: Europe's Forgotten Survivors*, pp. 104–5, Victor Golanz, used with permission from D. Logoreci (Logoreci, 1977)

Photograph 4 'Tito in discussion with his two chief lieutenants, Eduard Kardelj and Aleksander Rankovic, at some time during the mid-1960s' from *Tito*, pp. 320–1, Constable, used with permission from Hrvatski Povijesni Muzej, Zagreb (Ridley, 1994)

Photograph 5 'A New Year's Eve party in Yugoslavia at the end of 1967, attended by Tito and his wife Jovanka. Tito (though a Croat by ethnic origin) is wearing Serbian national costume for the occasion' from *Tito*, pp. 320–1, Constable, used with permission from Hrvatski Povijesni Muzej, Zagreb (Ridley, 1994)

We have been unable to trace the copyright holders for the following:

Photograph 6 'The resurgence of protest in Poland: a student demonstration in Warsaw, March 1968' from *The Struggles for Poland*, p. 176, Michael Joseph (Ascherson, 1987)

Photograph 7 'Alexander Dubcek acknowledges the crowd's enthusiasm for "socialism with a human face", Prague May Day 1968' from *Dubcek*, p. 111, Weidenfeld and Nicolson, 1970

Photograph 8 'Walter Ulbricht, the East German leader, visited Czechoslovakia on 12 August 1968. Here he is pictured presumably laying down the law to Dubcek about the risks entailed in his reform programme' from *Dubcek*, p. 175, Weidenfeld and Nicolson, 1970

# LIST OF ABBREVIATIONS

| | |
|---|---|
| ACCs | Allied Control Commissions |
| AK | Home Army |
| ÁVH | State Defence Authority |
| AVNOJ | Anti-Fascist Council of the People's Liberation of Yugoslavia |
| ÁVO | State Defence Department |
| CC | Central Committee |
| CMEA | Council for Mutual Economic Assistance |
| CPCz | Communist Party of Czechoslovakia |
| CPSU | Communist Party of the Soviet Union |
| CPY | Communist Party of Yugoslavia |
| DGSP | General Directorate of Popular Security |
| GDR | German Democratic Republic |
| HCP | Hungarian Communist Party |
| HSWP | Hungarian Socialist Workers' Party |
| HWP | Hungarian Workers' Party |
| JZD | Unified Agricultural Cooperative |
| KBW | Corps for Internal Security |
| KGB | Committee for State Security |
| KPD | Communist Party of Germany |
| KRN | National Council of the Homeland |
| KSRs | Conferences of Workers' Self-Management |
| LCY | League of Communists of Yugoslavia |
| LPG | Agricultural Production Cooperative |
| MEFESZ | Federation of Hungarian University and College Students' Associations |
| MGB | Ministry of State Security |
| NKVD | People's Commissariat for Internal Affairs |
| NSZ | National Armed Forces |
| OZNA | Bureau for the People's Protection |
| PKWN | Polish Committee of National Liberation |
| PPR | Polish Workers' Party |
| PPS | Polish Socialist Party |
| PSL | Polish Peasant Party |

| | |
|---|---|
| PZPR | Polish United Workers' Party |
| ROH | Revolutionary Trade Union Movement |
| SBZ | Soviet Occupation Zone |
| SED | Socialist Unity Party of Germany |
| SL | Peasant Party |
| SPD | Social Democratic Party of Germany |
| StB | State Security |
| TOZ | Association for the Joint Cultivation of the Land |
| UB | Security Office |
| UDBA | Administration of State Security |
| USSR | Union of Soviet Socialist Republics |
| WRN | Freedom, Equality, Independence |
| ZSL | United Peasant Party |

*Map 1*   Eastern Europe, 1945–91

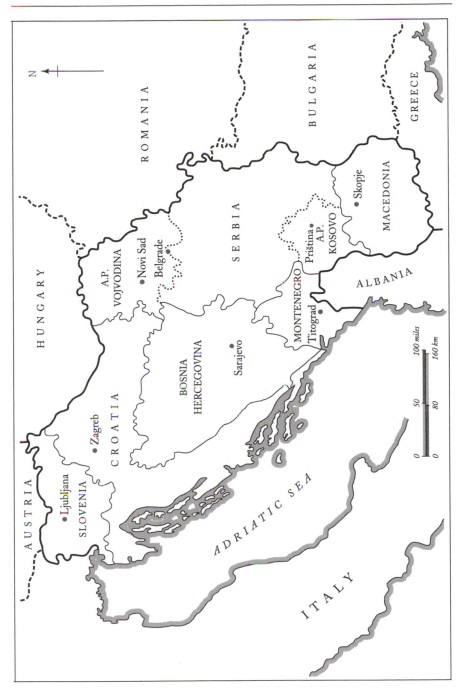

*Map 2* Yugoslavia, 1945–91

# PART ONE INTRODUCTION

# CHAPTER ONE

# GENERAL BACKGROUND

The general framework for the history of post-1945 Eastern Europe was set by three major elements: the international context, the local situation (in other words the historical inheritance of the region) and, finally, because the communists came to power everywhere and were also marked by their past, the evolution of the communist movement. We shall deal with these three points in that order.

## THE INTERNATIONAL CONTEXT

The logic of the Soviet victory in the Second World War was generally accepted by the Western allies. There was no wish to challenge Stalin on Eastern Europe in 1945, even though Western statesmen were often extremely critical of his actions. There is some evidence that the British Prime Minister, Winston Churchill, was ready to meet Stalin more than half way on the issue of Soviet influence there. In October 1944 he went to Moscow and made an agreement which essentially preserved Greece for the West (dividing influence there 90 to 10 per cent) in return for assigning a paramount position to the Soviet Union in Romania (90/10) and Bulgaria (75/25) and dividing Hungary and Yugoslavia equally. Two days later, after some hard bargaining between the British and Soviet Foreign Ministers, Anthony Eden and Viacheslav Molotov, Western influence in Hungary was brought down from 50 per cent to 20 per cent, and in Bulgaria from 25 per cent to 10 per cent [52 *pp.* 378–82].

The essence of the Churchill–Stalin 'spheres of influence' agreement of October 1944 was preserved in practice, though it was never confirmed by the United States. In theory, the Americans rejected the whole concept of a division of spheres of influence. Even so, American reactions to Stalin's moves between 1944 and 1947 were limited to complaints, followed by grudging acceptance, for without a willingness to use military force it was impossible to alter the situation. Stalin was ready to provide face-saving concessions, which were, however, more apparent than real. Thus the response to US Secretary of State James F. Byrnes's complaints at the December 1945

Moscow Conference about the composition of the Romanian and Bulgarian governments was that Stalin and Molotov accepted American proposals to change their composition [45; 46]. All this meant was that two powerless members of non-communist parties (Hațieganu and Romniceanu) were added to the Romanian government, and it was immediately recognized by the West; things took a little longer in Bulgaria because the opposition refused to join the government, but the end result was still the same: the West recognized communist-dominated governments [105; 175]. On 10 February 1947 the United States and Britain joined the Soviet Union in signing peace treaties in Paris with Hungary, Bulgaria and Romania, thereby giving up the one card they still had in their hands.

It must be stressed that the Western governments had very little alternative. They were in no position to challenge Soviet control on the ground. They felt they could achieve something on behalf of the non-communists by insisting that they be allowed to participate in coalition governments; in this respect, however, they were pushing at an open door, since this was exactly in line with Stalin's policies. The Yugoslav communists, however, did not favour coalitions. The British Prime Minister Winston Churchill insisted that their leader, Tito, should enter a coalition with Dr. Šubašić, the head of the exiled royal Yugoslav government (October 1944); but no attempt was made to specify how many ministers each side would be entitled to. Churchill was well aware that in making this agreement he was abandoning King Peter of Yugoslavia, and that the country would probably come under communist rule. Fitzroy Maclean, Chief of the Allied Military Mission to the Yugoslav communist partisans during the war, reported the following somewhat cynical discussion with Churchill on the subject:

> I emphasized that ... Tito and the other leaders of the Partisan Movement were openly and avowedly Communists and that the system which they would establish would inevitably be on Soviet lines. ... The Prime Minister's reply resolved my doubts. 'Do you intend to make Yugoslavia your home after the war?' 'No, Sir' I replied. 'Neither do I', he said. 'And, that being so, the less you and I worry about the form of government they set up, the better.' [59 *pp. 254–5*]

Later on, we shall examine how this extremely favourable international context was exploited by the communist parties of Eastern Europe in their bid for power after 1945.

## THE BURDEN OF HISTORY

We shall now look briefly at the main features of the domestic situation in Eastern Europe on the eve of the Second World War. Economically speaking, the main distinguishing feature of the region, in the historical context, was its undeveloped character, at least in comparison with Western

Europe. This contrast between East and West had arisen long before the twentieth century. It was not even a creation of the industrial revolution. Eastern Europe began to be differentiated from the West during the later Middle Ages, as a result of the continuing stagnation of its agriculture, and the late development and long persistence of serfdom in the East [*66 pp. 42–3*]. These points do not apply to East Germany or the westernmost part of Czechoslovakia, the mixed Czech–German province of Bohemia, which underwent agricultural and industrial revolutions at the same time as Western Europe [*66 pp. 70, 76*]. Unsurprisingly, these two areas were not regarded as part of Eastern Europe until they came under communist control after 1945.

There was also a division within Eastern Europe between the north western and south eastern zones of the region. As Paul Shoup has put it, 'as one moved east (and south) indices of births and child mortality rose; the percentage of the population employed in agriculture increased; and the degree of overpopulation in the countryside grew greater' [*50 p. 343*]. The south eastern zone is commonly referred to as the Balkans, although most people in the area are unhappy with the connotations of this word. Only the Bulgarians, writes Maria Todorova, are prepared to consider 'a Balkan name and a Balkan identity', and even they are 'ambiguous' about it [*95 p. 57*]. We shall therefore stick to the term 'South Eastern Europe'. This covers present-day Romania, Bulgaria, Albania and Greece and parts of former Yugoslavia. South Eastern Europe fell even further behind the West than the rest of Eastern Europe after the Middle Ages. This was probably a result of the Ottoman conquest of the fourteenth and fifteenth centuries, which destroyed the position of the native aristocracy. The economies of this region were based on small-scale peasant farming rather than the big landownership which prevailed further north. The subsequent predominance of small peasant farms did not assist economic growth. For the next three centuries there was a complete absence of population growth, which in premodern times, though not now, can be seen as a measure of economic development [*66 p. 184*].

The relatively undeveloped character of Eastern Europe was not substantially affected by the first signs of an economic take-off there, which appeared in the late nineteenth and early twentieth centuries. In the interwar years Eastern Europe continued to suffer from generally lower levels of what is normally described as 'infrastructure': housing availability, communications, transport, health care and education. A systematic comparison of the statistics for these indicators by Éva Ehrlich and her Budapest colleagues has made it clear that all the countries of Eastern Europe were placed in 1937 behind all Western European countries, with minor exceptions. Czechoslovakia, in eighteenth overall position, was closest to Western European levels; Romania, twenty-sixth, was furthest away. Greece, which also counted as part of Eastern Europe at that stage, was placed twenty-second [*79 p. 326*].

The situation is brought into still sharper focus by some of the detailed comparative figures. In the area of communications, Eastern Europe had 8.3 telephones per 1,000 people in 1937, Western Europe 70.6. In housing, as late as 1950, Eastern Europe had 1.9 persons per room, Western Europe 1.1. In health care there was also a pronounced gap. Infant mortality in 1937 was 143.5 per 1,000 live births in Eastern Europe, 61.6 per 1,000 in the West. Even after surviving the first year of life, Eastern Europeans still had a shorter life expectancy than people in the West. The gap was 5.3 years in 1929; by 1950 it had narrowed but was still 3.7 years. The continuing inadequacy of medical provision in 1950 is shown by contrasts in the availability of professional medical care: there were 0.52 doctors per 1,000 people in Eastern Europe and 0.93 in Western Europe [79 *p. 352*]. In levels of education and culture the difference between Czechoslovakia, Hungary and Poland and their Western counterparts was not great, but there was a contrast between South Eastern Europe (34 per cent illiteracy in 1937 and 10 radios per 1,000 people) and the countries further north (9.5 per cent illiteracy and 41 radios per 1,000 people) [79 *p. 258*]. Little progress had been made in closing this gap by 1948. Only in Yugoslavia and Hungary was there an increase in the proportion of children attending school (up from 46 per cent of the age group to 58 per cent in Yugoslavia, and 64 per cent to 83 per cent in Hungary). In Romania there was a decline (from 60 per cent to 42 per cent). In Bulgaria the proportion stayed at 54 per cent. Czechoslovakia also experienced a decline, from 96 per cent to 90 per cent [79 *pp. 96, 101*].

So history had given Eastern Europe a bad start economically and socially. But there was worse: the region did not, until 1918, have the chance to develop the homogeneous nations that had emerged in the West over time. Repeated waves of settlement and conquest created a patchwork of national groups, and a set of rival claims to the same territory. National differences were compounded (and sometimes actually created) by religious adherence. Thus a Hungarian would be Protestant or Catholic; while a Romanian would be Orthodox or Uniate. A Turk would be Muslim. A Croat would be Catholic, a Serb Orthodox. These differences reached back far into the past. We do not need to consider here the many disputes, as many as there are nations, over the early medieval history of the region. The motives of the parties to these disputes are usually transparent. The aim is always to assert 'prior rights of ownership' of a particular piece of land; it is assumed that to prove prior settlement is to prove prior rights.

What is much more important is rather to give some account of the *status quo* before the population movements of the Second World War transformed it. There were twelve major national groups in the region: Greeks, Bulgarians, Romanians, Albanians, Hungarians, Poles, Czechs, Slovaks, Slovenes, Croats, Serbs and Montenegrins. By the end of the nineteenth century the first three had their own states; by the end of the First

World War the next three had followed suit. The situation of the other nations in the list was more complex. The closely related Czechs and Slovaks were combined together after 1918 in the state of 'Czechoslovakia'; the Slovenes, Croats, Serbs and Montenegrins together made up 'Yugoslavia', a state which was based on the alleged 'unity of the South Slavs'. But the Slovenes were divided by language from the Croats and Serbs; the Croats were divided from the Serbs by religion, script and a long history of separate development. Moreover, some people argued that two further nations should be added to the Yugoslav list: the Macedonians and the Bosnian Muslims. The Macedonians were divided from the Bulgarians by rather subtle linguistic and cultural differences (many Bulgarians claimed them for themselves); the Bosnian Muslims were divided from the surrounding Croats and Serbs by religion and communal tradition, though not by language. The Yugoslav communists subsequently recognized the separate existence of both these nations [193 *pp. 114, 216*].

None of the eight states which constituted Eastern Europe after 1945 was entirely homogeneous. They all had their national minorities. There were compact minorities of Hungarians living on lands taken from historic Hungary after 1918 and added to Yugoslavia, Romania and Czechoslovakia; there were Turks in Bulgaria; there were Ukrainians and Lithuanians in Poland; there were Sorbs in East Germany; and there were large minorities of other nations spread over the whole area. In descending order of importance, these minorities were Germans, Jews, Roma (Gypsies), Vlachs, Greeks and Armenians [31; 41]. By 1946 the picture had been somewhat simplified by the Nazi extermination of most of the Eastern European Jews during the Second World War, and the expulsion of almost all Germans from the region after it. This reduced the two most important minorities to fragmentary remnants. But the others remained, and the national mosaic hardly seemed to have lost its complexity [41 *pp. 261–7*; 31 *pp. 209–10*].

The features we have outlined above are an essential background, without which it is impossible to explain the peculiarities of the Eastern European situation. Politically, Eastern Europe was marked (outside Czechoslovakia) by a lack of democratic traditions and a tendency towards authoritarianism. Socially, the domination of landowning and bureaucratic elites was hardly challenged. Culturally, the values and attitudes held by the population continued to be deeply traditional, though they were beginning to be covered by a thin veneer of Western-influenced intellectual life.

All this was hardly changed at all by the brief interwar period of independence. Most of the post-1918 rulers of Eastern Europe were less interested in radical change than in maintaining their own personal power and guaranteeing their nation's survival. Their attitudes were profoundly undemocratic, since they belonged to a bureaucratic political class which used the newly introduced system of parliamentary democracy as a barrier against change rather than an instrument of reform. The Eastern European countries, which started off as democracies, gradually fell into the hands of authoritarian or semi-authoritarian rulers under the impact of economic and ethnic tensions which they were skilled at manipulating [53 p. 20]. The exception was Czechoslovakia, where democracy survived until the state itself was broken up from outside in 1939 [127 p. 19].

In the economic sphere, there was some progress between the wars in absolute terms, but not in relation to the West. Using an average of the performance of six Western European countries between 1926 and 1934 to provide a bench-mark index of 100, Andrew Janos found that respective levels of national income during that period were Czechoslovakia 57, Hungary 45, Yugoslavia 41, Poland 35, Bulgaria 32, and Romania 30 [40 p. 152]. The gap in industrial development was even wider. In 1938 the whole of Eastern Europe produced 8 per cent of Europe's industrial output; the other 92 per cent was produced by Western Europe. Wartime devastation meant that there was no improvement either in industry or in agriculture in the next ten years. Relative levels were actually lower in 1948. Taking the United Kingdom index as 100, Czechoslovakia's national income was now 49, Poland's 35, Hungary's 24 and Bulgaria's 16 [79 p. 372].

These general comments should serve to give some impression of the historical burden resting on the Eastern Europeans at the outbreak of the Second World War. There were of course considerable variations from country to country. The region was very diverse. More detailed analyses are available both in general textbooks [32; 39; 53; 59; 79] and in various national histories [107; 108; 127; 147; 148; 167; 178; 184; 189].

## THE COMMUNIST PARTIES OF EASTERN EUROPE AND THE WARTIME VICTORY OF THE ALLIES

The intellectuals of Eastern Europe were uncomfortably aware of all the ways in which their region differed from the more fortunate West. This perception had an impact on political objectives, and on the prospects for communism after 1945. Modernization was seen as an important task, and this helped to increase support for the communist parties, which were seen among other things as bringing progress. The authoritarianism of communist doctrine was not necessarily a disadvantage. In many parts of Eastern Europe, authoritarian movements in favour of modernization were a feature of the 1930s. In Bulgaria, the Zveno* movement favoured a centralized state, a rationalized bureaucracy and state intervention to promote favoured industrial sectors [108 pp. 98–101]. Though Zveno were only briefly in power (they seized control in May 1934 but King Boris got rid of them a year later), the ideas of the movement continued to be implemented by the royal dictatorship of the later 1930s. In Romania, the Liberal Party leader

Gheorghe Tătărescu combined support for the royal dictatorship of King Carol II with a programme of rapid industrialization, to be achieved with government support through fiscal protection and bank loans [59 p. 132]. The communists took over and absorbed some of these aspirations after 1945. They even entered into temporary alliances with some of the groups that advocated them. In Romania, Tătărescu was brought into the government; in Bulgaria, the first Fatherland Front government contained five members of Zveno.

In Hungary, the Populist movement of the 1930s advocated radical land reform, and the socio-economic transformation of the country. They regarded the nature of the governmental system as a matter of indifference, provided the government served the interests of the peasantry. The Populists found a temporary home later in the Hungarian communist party [72 p. 74].

The communists shared the objectives of modernization outlined above, but their situation was made much more complex by their international connections. Their primary task was not to improve the situation of their own country, but to defend the Soviet Union and, as loyal members of the Communist International, to obey its instructions. Policies were established in Moscow and applied internationally with little regard to the local situation in the interwar and wartime period. This historical background has been examined both for Europe as a whole [27; 30; 49; 57] and for specific communist parties [104; 118; 133; 150; 159; 177; 180]. At every twist and turn in the Communist International's interwar policy the current party leaders were obliged either to swallow their words and act against their former convictions or to enter into opposition to the general line set by the centre, with the inevitable consequence of expulsion from the movement. This does much to explain the slavish way in which the surviving communist leaders imitated Soviet practices and Soviet policies when they were in a position of power after 1945.

It is tempting, but inaccurate, to describe them as nothing but Soviet agents. Norman Davies, for instance, remarks that 'Bierut (the head of the Polish communist party) was a stool-pigeon of the most obvious ilk' [157 p. 573]. Although there is evidence that some communists reported on their colleagues to local Soviet representatives, who then in turn reported back to Moscow [Doc. 10], those who made up the public face of communism had placed their faith voluntarily in the Stalinist version of communism; they genuinely believed that the way forward for human society lay in the direction of dictatorial, modernizing regimes in which society was merged with the state, and an all-powerful party controlled the course of events. Alongside 'true believers' of this kind, there were people like Wolfgang Leonhard, who rose to a high position in the KPD* (the German communist party) and its East German successor the SED* before he decided to defect to the West. Such people were likely to suffer from attacks of the 'political collywobbles' because they combined a belief in communism with the expectation that it could somehow develop differently outside the Soviet Union, that there could be more political participation by ordinary people and that the violent and ruthless terrorism that marred Soviet communism would prove unnecessary further West [12 *p. 382*].

Between 1939 and 1941 the communists of Eastern Europe did their best to avoid getting involved in the conflict between Hitler and the West. The Comintern line was that this was a war between rival groups of imperialists, in which neither side should be supported. In June 1941, with the German invasion of the Soviet Union, all this changed. An all-out fight against the Nazi invaders, and collaboration with anyone who was prepared to help, was the new policy (although there had been a certain amount of communist resistance to Nazi occupation in Eastern Europe before June 1941, especially in Yugoslavia) [57 *p. 171*].

The formation of broad anti-Fascist coalitions was a tactic laid down by the highest communist authorities in Moscow, on instructions from Stalin. These coalitions were to be 'National Fronts' drawing in as wide a spectrum of political opinion as possible. The only qualification for membership in these fronts was a genuine readiness to resist Nazism and Fascism. All divisive issues were to be put to one side [57 *p. 178*]. The size and effectiveness of the national front coalitions varied according to the situation in each country. Sometimes the non-communists rejected the outstretched hand with contumely; sometimes they grasped it in warm friendship. In Czechoslovakia, the second variant prevailed. There the coalition was both broad and effective; there were strong reasons for cooperation, ranging from the feeling that Britain and France had betrayed the Czechs at Munich in 1938 to traditional ideas of Slav solidarity with the Soviet Union, alongside a hard-headed sense of geopolitical realities. In Bulgaria too, the Fatherland Front, set up definitively by the communists in 1942 after a false start the previous year, was able to draw in some Social Democrats, the left wing of the Agrarians under Nikola Petkov and the Zveno group under Kimon Georgiev. Other Bulgarian political groups, such as the Pastukhov faction of Social Democracy and Nikola Mushanov's Democratic Party, refused to join, but the Fatherland Front was at least broadly representative of left-wing opinion in the country [107 *p. 178*].

In Poland and Romania the opposite situation prevailed. Here the Soviet Union was the national enemy, and in addition had just annexed large parts of each country. In both countries the communists insisted that the new boundaries must be accepted. Bessarabia, taken from Romania by Stalin in 1940, had to stay part of the Soviet Union, said the Romanian communist party. This considerably reduced the number of Romanian coalition partners [177 *p. 37*]. Hence the National Democratic Front, set up in October 1944, consisted of the communists, the Social Democrats, and two organizations controlled by the communists, the Ploughmen's Front and the Union of Patriots. All the other independent non-communist parties stayed outside [175 *p. 99*]. It was claimed subsequently by the communist leader Gheorghiu-Dej that a faction within the party, led by his rivals Ana Pauker and Vasile Luca, was opposed to the policy of creating a broad national front. They would have preferred to ignore the other parties and simply seize power, relying on the support of the Red Army [177 *p. 43*]. If true, this would be surprising, given that, as 'Muscovite' communists, Pauker and Luca would have been well aware of Stalin's preference for broad fronts at this time. Unfortunately there is no contemporary evidence either way.

In Poland, the omens for a broad national front coalition were never favourable, for similar reasons. The occupation of Eastern Poland by the Soviet Union in 1939, followed by its division into three parts and forcible inclusion in the Soviet republics of Ukraine and Belorussia, and the Republic of Lithuania, was not accepted by most Poles. The PPR*, however, was obliged to defend these new boundaries. Worse still, the Soviet security organs had massacred thousands of Polish army officers in 1940, burying them in the Katyn forest. When the German government revealed in 1943 that it had discovered their mass graves, the Soviet authorities naturally denied everything, but the Poles tended not to believe this. We now know they were right.

The Katyn issue led to a complete break between the exiled Polish government in London and the Soviet Union, which meant in turn that no party affiliated with London was prepared to join the National Council of the Homeland (KRN)* the PPR set up in December 1943. Even the left-wingers who had split off from the Polish Socialist Party in January 1943 were mainly opposed to cooperating with the communists. A few individual non-communists joined the KRN, but it was essentially a communist body. The Poles in Moscow, who were more in tune with Stalin's thinking than the communists on the spot in Poland, made desperate efforts to widen the coalition by watering down the rather radical statements in the KRN's Manifesto of December 1943 in favour of the nationalization of industry and the expropriation of large estates [*Doc. 3*]. The Manifesto of the PKWN*, issued on 22 July 1944, restricted nationalization to large German-owned enterprises. Small and medium-sized firms would remain in private hands. Similarly, the expropriation of land was limited to estates owned by Germans and collaborators [16 *p. 23*]. It was all to no avail. The only additional ally they gained was a new faction of the Peasant Party (SL)* established by the communists themselves [36 *pp. 7–9*].

In Hungary, it proved possible to establish a fairly wide National Independence Front. It included, alongside the Communists, members of the Social Democratic, Smallholder, National Peasant and Citizens' Democratic parties. The first programme of the National Independence Front, issued in

November, was too radical for Moscow's taste. It included the nationalization of energy producers and insurance companies and the placing of industrial cartels under state supervision. When the Hungarian communists discussed these matters with Stalin, Molotov and other Soviet leaders in December, Stalin insisted that the programme should be changed 'to underline more strongly the defence of private property and the preservation and development of private enterprise'. And he added: 'Declare especially clearly that private property remains, in parallel with the Polish manifesto.' Furthermore, the Hungarian communist leaders, who had spent the war in the Soviet Union, should not enter the government because 'they will be considered Moscow puppets'. The new government would have to be led by generals who had supported the Horthy regime 'because they will be respected by the Hungarian officer corps' [46 *p. 316*]. This advice was followed. The new government had as its Prime Minister, Defence Minister and Food Supply Minister three generals from the former regime of Admiral Horthy, which had ruled Hungary until October 1944. The rest of it was composed of second-line communists, local rather than Muscovite, and of Smallholder and Social Democratic politicians. The government programme was studiously moderate.

Hungary, Czechoslovakia and Bulgaria were the only countries where it was possible to achieve the kind of broad national front that Stalin had in mind. We have already outlined the problems that came up in Poland and Romania. In Albania and Yugoslavia, rival resistance movements came into existence during the war, and despite Moscow's earnest wish that cooperation at ground level should reflect the cooperation established internationally between the Soviet Union and the Western powers, these movements came into conflict with each other very rapidly.

In Yugoslavia, the year 1941 saw the emergence of two deadly rivals: the *četnici\**, led by Draža Mihailović, who gave their allegiance to the exiled royal government of King Peter, and the communist partisans, led by Josip Broz Tito. The latter were committed by the Communist International's national front strategy, launched in response to the Nazi invasion of the Soviet Union in June 1941, to attempting to secure cooperation and joint action with any force genuinely fighting against Nazism and Fascism. But a conference between Tito and Mihailović in September 1941 failed to arrive at any agreement, and armed conflict between the two sides began in November. It never stopped. Yugoslavia was the scene in the next four years of a three-cornered struggle which pitted against each other the communists, the *četnici*, and the Axis forces of the Germans and Italians, backed up by various local collaborators, in particular the Croat *ustaše\** (rebels), under their leader Ante Pavelić. Both the communists and the *četnici* succumbed to the temptation to put their own fratricidal conflict first, and the anti-Nazi cause second, but while Tito's offer of March 1943 was rejected by the

Germans and did not come to light until long after the war [195 *p. 28*], Mihailović's collaboration with the Axis was common knowledge and led in 1944 to a decision by both Britain and the United States to withdraw support from him, and concentrate military aid on the communist partisans, even though, as we have seen, the Western powers were fully aware that Tito and his followers intended to establish a communist regime in Yugoslavia after they had defeated the Nazi occupying forces.

In Albania, as in Yugoslavia, the communists attempted to forge a broad-based resistance movement after 1941. For the next two years the communist National Liberation Movement fought side by side with a monarchist guerrilla movement based on the clan chieftains of the north and north east of the country, which was led by Abas Kupi, a former officer in the royal army. But in November 1943 Kupi broke with the communists. A civil war ensued, ending with Kupi's defeat in 1944. In the south a nationalist movement called *Balli Kombëtar* (National Front) was set up in 1942. It too cooperated initially with the communist National Liberation Movement. Fighting broke out between these ill-assorted allies after August 1943. One of the issues that divided *Balli Kombëtar* from the communists was their attitude to Kosovo; because the communists relied heavily on Yugoslav support they had to advocate the inclusion of Kosovo in Yugoslavia, whereas *Balli Kombëtar* wanted to keep the province within Albania (Hitler had attached it to Albania after the fall of Yugoslavia in 1941) [189 *pp. 72–83*].

The victory of the communists in Yugoslavia and Albania over all their local opponents resulted from a combination of unique factors: sheer good fortune (the collapse of Italian Fascism and the resultant creation of a power vacuum in Italian-occupied Yugoslavia), inadvertent German aid (the German forces wiped out many of the non-communist Albanian guerrillas), Western aid (given mainly to the communists on the assumption that they were fighting the Italians and Germans more effectively), the discrediting of all alternatives, and finally, the communists' own discipline and determination and the military experience many of them had gained in the Spanish Civil War [54 *pp. 56–7*; 188 *pp. 213–22*]. In the next chapter we shall examine the reasons for the success of the communists in the rest of Eastern Europe.

# CHAPTER TWO

## THE SEIZURE OF POWER

REASONS FOR THE COMMUNISTS' SUCCESS

The communist seizure of power in Eastern Europe was accomplished with relative ease. There are several reasons for this. The impact of the Second World War is one. This weakened the forces of resistance to communism. Direct military conquest by the Red Army in the course of 1944 and 1945 removed the Nazis and their allies from the scene. Right-wing governments and movements in Eastern Europe had generally collaborated with the Axis during the Second World War, partly because they shared with the Nazis and Fascists a hatred of communism, partly because Hitler cleverly offered political benefits (such as semi-independence for Slovakia and Croatia, and gains of territory for Bulgaria, Hungary and Romania). The political left (the socialists and some of the agrarian movements) tended to share communist objectives or at least not to see communism as the main danger.

Poland is the one country of Eastern Europe where the Right did not collaborate with the Axis. Here a strong anti-communist force arose on a national basis: the Home Army (AK)*. It would have been much more difficult to seize power there if the Home Army had not made the terrible tactical mistake of launching the Warsaw Uprising in 1944 [157 p. 475]. Stalin may have deliberately kept the Red Army out of the fight for the city; but in any case an advance on Warsaw did not fit in with his military priorities, which were dictated by the impending Soviet invasion of the Balkans. Whether intentional or not, the final result of Soviet actions was to nullify the calculation the Home Army leaders had made when they ordered the rising: they hoped to be able to play a part in determining Poland's future by negotiating from the strong position of leaders of a successful uprising. Instead, the insurgents, after a heroic struggle, were defeated by the Nazi forces. The Home Army was decimated, although not completely destroyed, since many of its units remained outside Warsaw.

Apart from bringing the Red Army to Eastern Europe, the Second World War also had a more subtle result. During the five years of Nazi occupation the indigenous middle classes were expropriated (and in some cases physically liquidated) for the benefit of the war economy of the Third Reich. Industries were taken over by the state, and 'local economies were redirected away from the West' [51 *p. 22*]. Jan Gross's arguments on this point are generally persuasive, although he exaggerates the continuity of economic planning and state control in Bulgaria, where the wartime alliance with Nazi Germany did not really provide any basis for communist industrialization. In fact the spread of small-scale enterprises (their number increased by one-third during the war) and the decline of the state sector (it fell from 9 per cent in 1939 to 5 per cent in 1944) actually worked in the opposite direction [108 *pp. 115–18*].

In various ways, therefore, the Second World War contributed power-fully to clearing the way to a communist takeover. When it came, the seizure of power had almost nothing in common with the classic revolutions, the French one of 1789 or the Russian one of February 1917. In terms of method it was more reminiscent of the Fascist coups of the interwar years: use of the power of a state which had already been penetrated from within, cheered on by a mass movement whose role was reduced to confirming and validating a process that had already taken place. The main driving force behind the postwar communist *coups d'état* never lay in the streets, though there was no shortage of communist street demonstrations in the next few years.

There are some differences of opinion in the literature about the precise balance between the role of mass action and that of the local army and police, backed up where necessary by the army and police of the Soviet Union. We shall examine the role of Soviet policy later in this chapter. First, however, we shall look at the reasons why there might be popular support for communism after 1945. The victory of the Red Army brought with it a tremendous growth in the strength and attractiveness of communist parties [*Doc. 28*]. In the first place there were inevitably careerist reasons for supporting a party which was already in power, or was very likely to come to power in the future. In some countries the growth in numbers was highly dramatic. In Bulgaria, the party grew twentyfold between 1944 and 1948. Here the new recruits were more often peasants than workers [113 *p. 112*]. There was also support outside the ranks of the communists for a more vaguely conceived set of political and social changes, which many on the left thought the communists would bring about.

The communist parties also provided a political home for members of the national minorities, where they existed. This was natural, as the com-munists had until then been the most consistent opponents of chauvinism and anti-Semitism, even to the extent of taking sides against the national claims of the state in which they were organizing (most notably between 1928 and 1934, when this was prescribed by the ultra-left line of the Communist International) [180 *pp. 60–1*]. The evidence for the view that national minorities tended to support the communists after 1945 is admittedly impressionistic, but it is widely shared. In Hungary, says Kovrig, 'many of the new intellectual recruits were Jewish' and 'many survivors' of the Holocaust 'gravitated to the communist party' [150 *pp. 167–8*]. Jews also preponderated in the top Hungarian leadership (Mátyás Rákosi, Mihály Farkas, Ernő Gerő and József Révai ran the communist party until 1953). In Romania 'the top leadership of the communist party consisted until 1952 of members of ethnic minorities, Jews in particular' [33 *p. 278*]. With 4 per cent of the total population, Jews made up 18 per cent of the party membership in the 1930s [179 *p. 26*]. In Poland, the survivors of the Holocaust flocked to join the PPR, and several party leaders were Jewish (including Jakub Berman and Hilary Minc). The Polish communist leader Władysław Gomułka referred in a letter to Stalin to the 'high percentage of Jews in the state and party apparatus' [*Doc. 14*]. In Yugoslavia, a state where every nation was a minority somewhere, the communist party was the only organization which spanned the national divide. We shall examine this point in more detail later.

Perhaps paradoxically, the communist parties also gained support by making use of the national feeling of majority communities. Everywhere after 1945 they took the lead in policies of expulsion of unwelcome national minorities. In the main this applied to Germans, who were compactly settled in parts of Poland and Czechoslovakia and spread more thinly over Romania and Yugoslavia before the war. But in principle it could happen to others (such as Hungarians). There were two ways of dealing with minorities: to give them equal rights and perhaps even autonomy (the Hungarians benefited from this in Romania) or to remove them through 'transfer' abroad.

'Transfer' was the preferred method of dealing with German minorities. It was provided for under clause thirteen of the Potsdam Agreements of 1945. It was approved by all the political parties, although the communists gained most of the political credit for the measure. The main organized transfers took place in 1946. They affected about five million Germans in Poland, and two million in Czechoslovakia [157 *p. 563*; 127 *p. 31*]. The Czech National Socialist politician Hubert Ripka visited Stalin in March 1946 and appealed for his support in enabling the continuing transfer of Sudeten Germans to take place, because the Americans had stopped accepting them into their occupation zone of South West Germany. Stalin agreed that they could enter East Germany instead.

In Slovakia, the communist leaders Clementis and Husák successfully outbid the Slovak Democrats over the issue of the expulsion of the Magyar minority [34 *p. 128*]. This led to a conflict with the Hungarian government. In January 1946 the Hungarian communist leaders Gerő and Révai complained about the Slovak treatment of the local Magyars, on the basis that it was contrary to Marxist national policy. The Slovaks replied that they preferred to follow 'the living practice, Stalin' rather than the 'dogmatic, theoretical arguments' of the Hungarians [41 *p. 54*]. Many Hungarians (Magyars) were forced to leave their homes and go south to Hungary proper. In Bulgaria, where 80,000 Jews had survived the Second World War, the new government encouraged them to leave after 1945, and most did so. Many members of the Turkish minority in Bulgaria were pushed south across the border into Turkey. Finally, the Bulgarians dealt with the Macedonian problem, but in the opposite way: they moved the Macedonians away from the border with Yugoslavia to the interior of the country [113 *p. 105*]. The ostensible goal in all these cases was to achieve maximum national homogeneity, but the communists' real objective, in which they succeeded, was to gain popularity.

For all the above reasons, the communist parties of Eastern Europe underwent a great transformation between 1939 and 1945. Having started the war as rather small underground political sects, they had become mass organizations by the time that it ended. They went on increasing in size until they had seized power and swallowed up the Social Democrats. In this first postwar period, there was a deliberate policy of opening the party's gates as wide as possible. It was followed later on, during the 1950s, by severe pruning, in the context of the purges.

Despite these increases in communist support, there is no doubt about the vital role of the Red Army, and of direct Soviet intervention, in the communist seizure of power. The three exceptions are Albania, Czechoslovakia and Yugoslavia. In Albania and Yugoslavia, communist partisan movements came to power largely by their own efforts; in Czechoslovakia, the communists were in a commanding position from the start and the Red Army was not needed (it was withdrawn from the country in November 1945). Elsewhere it was a different matter. The three defeated enemy countries of Hungary, Bulgaria and Romania were at first not trusted to run themselves. Allied Control Commissions (ACCs)*, composed of Soviet, United States and British representatives, were set up to control the situation behind the scenes. The Soviet representative was always the dominant partner. In Bulgaria, General S.S. Biriuzov described himself as the 'Soviet viceroy'. He reported directly to Moscow and made decisions without even informing his British and American counterparts. In November 1944 he forbade the Bulgarian government to communicate with them; in January 1945 he compelled the Agrarians to remove the obstinate Dr G.M. Dimitrov from his position as party leader, by threatening to dissolve the party if they did not do so [105 *p. 91*]. When the West's representatives in Bulgaria objected to his methods, Biriuzov simply suspended all sessions of the ACC. By the time they resumed (in August 1945) the main decisions which placed the communists on the road to power had already been made [105 *p. 69*].

General V.P. Vinogradov, the Soviet head of the ACC in Romania, behaved similarly. He supported the agitation of the communist-run National Democratic Front for the removal of the National Liberal and National Peasant parties from the coalition government and the appointment of communists as ministers. He got his way (November 1944). Even stronger Soviet pressure was needed, in the shape of two visits from Andrei Vyshinsky, one of the top men in the Soviet government, to bring about the next stage in the communist campaign for control of Romania. Vyshinsky first imposed a communist under-secretary at the Ministry of the Interior (December 1944) then got rid of the existing government altogether, forcing King Michael to dismiss his Prime Minister, General Rădescu, and appoint Dr Petru Groza, head of the Ploughmen's Front and a close associate of the communists (March 1945). The British and American representatives in Bucharest themselves advised surrender: 'Disturbing as the situation is', wrote Sir Orme Sargent, 'I cannot see what more could be done. The Soviet representative is backed by Soviet military force' [6 *p. 489*]. The American President, Franklin D. Roosevelt, took the same view: 'Romania is not a good place for a test case', he wrote [5 *p. 510*].

In Hungary, the other former enemy country, the Soviet representative on the ACC, Marshal K.E. Voroshilov, had an equally dominant position. His initial abstention from political intervention can easily be explained: the Hungarian communists seemed to have things under control, having formed a coalition of the main democratic political forces. In addition, Stalin's attitude was probably affected by the October 1944 percentage agreement with Churchill, which gave the West a greater role in Hungary than in Bulgaria or Romania. Late in 1945, however, the situation began to slip out of the control of the Hungarian Communist Party (HCP)*. On 7 October, the city of Budapest went to the polls. The Workers' Unity Front, which combined communists and social democrats on a single ticket, received 43 per cent of the vote; but their opponents, the Smallholders' Party, gained 51 per cent. It was clear that in any free national elections the Smallholders would win a majority. Voroshilov tried to prevent this by encouraging the formation of an electoral alliance, with a guarantee of 40 per cent of the seats for the Smallholders. This attempt failed, as the Western representatives resisted more firmly than they had done in Romania or Bulgaria.

After the stunning victory of the Smallholders in the national elections of 4 November 1945 (they gained 57 per cent of the vote, the communists and social democrats only 17 per cent apiece), Voroshilov again intervened, forcing them to continue in coalition with the communists and insisting on the key point that the communists must receive the Ministry of the Interior (it went to Imre Nagy). The party leader, Mátyás Rákosi, frankly admitted the importance of Voroshilov's role at this time: 'Now that we have the direct support of the Soviet Union, the outcome of the struggle cannot be doubted'

[150 *p. 182*]. The decisive role of Soviet support was confirmed by the outgoing United States representative on the ACC in June 1947, who reported that he had had 'no voice whatsoever in the control and direction of the government of Hungary. The Soviet chairman has directly and through the HCP daily taken unilateral actions' [8 *p. 324*].

## STALIN'S AIMS AND METHODS

Stalin's, and more generally, Soviet, aims in Eastern Europe are still not entirely clear, despite the recent release of many documents from the archives. A lot of light has been thrown on many episodes, but the question has not been definitively resolved. Historians have long been divided into camps on these issues, with 'cold warriors' at one end of the spectrum and 'revisionists' at the other. There is also material produced by Soviet and communist propagandists, both then and subsequently. Their version naturally stresses the role of popular action and ignores the pressure exerted by the Soviet Union and its agencies.

The most recent study, by Vojtech Mastny, written on the basis of newly available Soviet documentation, reaches the following categorical conclusion: 'Nowhere beyond what Moscow considered the Soviet borders did its policies foresee the establishment of communist regimes'. Mastny does, however, note that 'in the Eastern part of Europe' it was intended that 'the Soviet Union's influence would be paramount' whereas in the West there would be open political competition [45 *pp. 20–1*].

We have, however, already quoted evidence to show that in Romania and Bulgaria the Soviet Union used its position on the ACCs set up after the war to weight the scales in favour of the local communist parties. The Soviet Foreign Minister, Viacheslav Molotov, commented in September 1944 that the Western powers did not need to have any more influence in Romania than the Soviet Union did in Italy (which was very little). The Western representatives on the ACCs were reduced to powerless grumbling about Soviet actions. In Bulgaria, the already-mentioned Soviet representative General Biriuzov later described his role as 'to knock out of the hands of our (Western) partners the stick which they tried to insert into the wheel of history at every turn' [36 *p. 41*]. As we have seen, he repeatedly intervened in local politics.

Stalin seems to have taken the 'percentage agreement' of October 1944 with Churchill fairly seriously. He thought he had made a deal whereby he would restrain the Greek communists, while the West would not question what he did in Romania and Bulgaria. Stalin told Churchill on 18 July 1945 that he had been 'hurt by the American demand for a change of government in Romania and Bulgaria. He was not meddling in Greek affairs, and it was unjust of them' [59 *p. 285*].

The Moscow Conference decisions of December 1945 represented an apparent retreat by the Soviet leader. At that conference, the three Foreign Ministers (Soviet, British and American) recommended that the Romanian and Bulgarian governments be widened by the inclusion of two leaders from the non-communist opposition, and that, in Romania, free elections be held; these were all prerequisites for the signing of the peace treaties. The Bulgarian elections of November 1945, in which the opposition refused to participate because there would not be a free choice, were nevertheless recognized as valid by the British and American governments: they did not insist that Bulgaria hold a fresh ballot. In Romania, the opposition weakly agreed to the inclusion of two representatives in a government which was still entirely run by the communists (January 1946); but in Bulgaria, the Moscow Conference offer set off a round of political bargaining, for Nikola Petkov, the Agrarian leader, and Kosta Lulchev, the Social Democrat, were made of stronger stuff. They were determined not to enter the cabinet unless they were given real powers. In particular, they wanted the Ministries of Justice and the Interior to be turned over to them. Faced with this strong stand, the Fatherland Front government agreed to a compromise, by which the opposition received the Ministry of Justice and two under-secretaryships at the Ministry of the Interior; genuinely free elections would also be held. But Stalin now intervened to forbid the deal. In his view, the Bulgarian government had given far too much away. On 28 March 1946 the Soviet Ambassador, Stepan Kirsanov, demanded that the offer be withdrawn; Prime Minister Georgiev and his colleagues complied [7 *pp. 92–4*; 105 *p. 172*].

Soviet policy towards Czechoslovakia at the time of the coup of February 1948, which brought the communists to power, is another case in point. Valerian Zorin, the Soviet deputy Foreign Minister, was present in Prague throughout the February crisis. His advice to Gottwald was 'be firm; do not retreat before the Right and do not hesitate'. The impression he gives in his reports is that the Czechoslovak communist leaders were hesitant people, unwilling to take the initiative and rather apprehensive of a possible United States invasion if there were to be a communist coup. Zorin reported to Moscow that Gottwald 'exaggerated the difficulty of acting against the President' and that he had a 'fear and horror of breaking the formal provisions of the constitution'. Gottwald also suggested that it would have a helpful psychological effect 'if Soviet military detachments in Germany and Austria started to move towards the Czechoslovak border' [128 *pp. 58–9*]. It should be added that in this case Soviet help was hardly needed. With control of the police, the benevolent neutrality of the army, a strong and militant contingent of working-class supporters, and ineffectiveness and lack of determination on the part of their opponents, the Czechoslovak communists could come to power independently.

## THE PROCESS OF GAINING POWER

The techniques used by the communists to gain power did not vary fundamentally from country to country. The prior control of the police and the army through the Ministry of the Interior and the Ministry of Defence was one common factor. If we examine the composition of the coalition governments set up in 1944 and 1945, we find that the communist party almost always insisted on, and received, control of the police forces. Thus in Bulgaria, Anton Yugov, as Minister of the Interior, controlled the police and the militia; in Hungary, Imre Nagy was in charge of the police, including the secret police (known at this stage as the ÁVO*). Rákosi later recalled that 'the ÁVO was the only body over which we kept complete control, refusing to share it with the other parties of the coalition' [34 *p. 107*].

In Czechoslovakia, Václav Nosek was Minister of the Interior, and he used his powers to pack the central headquarters and the district commands of the police force with communists. By 1947 'the communist party was in almost complete control of the Ministry of the Interior and all its branches' [51 *p. 255*]. It was in fact the attempt by the National Socialists to reverse this position in February 1948 that set off the final crisis which ended in the communist seizure of power [36 *pp. 17, 21*]. In Poland, the Ministry of Public Security was held by the communist Stanisław Radkiewicz, while the Defence portfolio was held by Michał Rola-Żymierski who, though not a communist, acted entirely under their instructions [159 *p. 186*]. Where the communists did not at first have control of the police, as in Romania, this was the first target of their agitation, with Soviet backing. In March 1945 the government of Petru Groza was installed after weeks of political crisis marked by demonstrations and counter-demonstrations and strong pressure exerted on King Michael by Stalin's special envoy, Andrei Vyshinsky. In the new government, the communists held only three cabinet posts, but this time they made sure of the Ministry of the Interior, which was given to Teohari Georgescu.

One technique the communists made use of very effectively after 1945 was what could be called 'window-dressing': the masses were brought on to the stage as a means of pressure, though the true locus of decision-making lay elsewhere. The Romanian demonstrations of February 1945 are one example; a much better researched and better known one is the activities of the Action Committees of the National Front in Czechoslovakia in February 1948. They made a coup look like a revolution. But in fact the party 'limited the role of the working class in the making of the revolution, and restricted its capacity to act' afterwards [114 *p. 238*]. The sham of the February 1948 'revolution' was exposed by Czechoslovak historians themselves during the Prague Spring of 1968, though their revelations were quickly suppressed after the Soviet invasion, and any further examination of the subject was prohibited.

Undermining non-communist parties was another very effective technique of ensuring a smooth transition to sole power. There was a simple way to accomplish this. The non-communist parties usually contained some groups of people who favoured the new state of affairs. They could be seen as 'left wingers', although it would be more accurate to call them 'communist sympathizers', since their views were not always left-wing in terms of policy. These people were encouraged financially and in other ways. Here are some examples, taken from Czechoslovakia. In November 1947, the Communist Party of Czechoslovakia (CPCz)* set up a special department under Ota Hromádko which had the task of identifying leaders and establishing sections within non-communist parties which would be ready to take control or, failing that, split off, at the appropriate moment. The leader of the Social Democratic 'left' was Zdeněk Fierlinger; within the People's Party this role was played by Josef Plojhar; within the Slovak Democrats by Ján Ševčík. Alois Neumann, a left-wing member of the Czech National Socialists, was rewarded after the communist victory in February 1948 with the Ministry of Justice [55 *p. 99*]. The tactic of undermining the parties from within could only be effective if sympathizers were prevented from acting according to their convictions and joining the communist party; General Ludvík Svoboda, for instance, went to see Gottwald about leaving his party, and was directly advised to stay where he was. Even after February 1948 it continued to be necessary for left Social Democrats to stay within their party, to prepare the merger with the communist party [120 *p. 162*].

It was also possible to undermine non-communist parties from outside. This was the famous 'salami tactic'. The phrase was coined for Hungary in 1946 by Zoltán Pfeiffer, who was later to fall victim to the tactic himself when he was expelled from the Smallholders' Party. But the method was used in many other countries. The party in question was seen as a sausage, and its most extreme right end was sliced off; but then the next slice became exposed as the most right-wing element and was itself in turn sliced off [145 *p. 22*].

Political opponents who displayed extreme stubbornness could be dealt with by yet another method: the secret police could invent conspiracies. In Bulgaria, the resistance of the Agrarians was overcome in this way. In June 1947, Nikola Petkov and twenty-four other Agrarian deputies were arrested in the National Assembly for allegedly taking part in an 'armed plot' against the Fatherland Front government. Petkov's trial (August 1947) was quickly followed by his execution in September. In Romania, Iuliu Maniu and Ion Mihalache, leaders of the National Peasant Party, were tried along with seventeen others for allegedly conspiring with two American intelligence officers to organize a rising and set up American air bases in the country. The two main defendants were sentenced to life imprisonment [175 *pp. 134–6*]. In Hungary, Béla Kovács, leader of the Smallholders, was arrested in February 1947 and charged with spying for a Western intelligence service.

His fall was followed by that of Ferenc Nagy, the Hungarian Prime Minister, also a Smallholder, who was forced to resign in May 1947 after being warned that he too would be charged in connection with the same conspiracy [147 *p. 182*].

## THE YUGOSLAV EXCEPTION

Yugoslavia differed in so many ways from the rest of Eastern Europe that it has to be treated separately. The Communist Party of Yugoslavia (CPY)* itself was exceptional for three reasons: it was the only political group that genuinely rose above the ethnic discords that tore the country apart during the Second World War; it was overwhelmingly the most significant force of resistance to German and Italian rule; and it was genuinely independent of Moscow.

The first two points are easier to explain than the third. The ability of the party to bridge the ethnic gap arose from its multi-ethnic composition, both in terms of members and party leaders, the firm rejection during the war of any temptation to engage in a policy of national revenge and a political line which (on paper at least) stressed a federal rather than a centralistic solution to Yugoslavia's problems. The list of main party leaders speaks for itself: Josip Broz Tito and Andrija Hebrang were Croats, Milovan Djilas a Montenegrin, Aleksandar Ranković a Serb, Moše Pijade was Jewish and Edvard Kardelj a Slovene. The ethnic composition of the party at this time is not precisely known but the simultaneous conduct of the partisan struggle over most of the country made the CPY* different from other parties, which always had their base in a particular national group. In terms of regional membership it was relatively broadly based: in 1945, 28 per cent of members were located in Serbia, 36 per cent in Croatia, 11 per cent in Slovenia, 14 per cent in Bosnia-Herzegovina, 8 per cent in Montenegro and 4 per cent in Macedonia [193 *p. 269*]. Moreover, in 1937 the communist party itself had been partly federalized by the setting up of separate communist parties for Croatia and Slovenia [193 *p. 45*]. The leader of the Croat Communists, Hebrang, was able to compete effectively with other Croat political groups after 1941 by launching a struggle for Croat (as opposed to Yugoslav) national liberation, which he distinguished both from Ante Pavelić's pro-Axis policy and the Croat Peasant Party's approach, which was to wait until the end of the war. The Croat Peasant Party 'failed to develop any effective resistance movement of its own'. As a result of this 'the Partisans appeared to be attracting to their ranks a growing number of Croat Peasant Party adherents' [183 *p. 154*]. Despite Hebrang's stress on Croat national liberation, members of the Serbian minority also flocked to join the Partisans because they saw them as the sole real protection against the atrocities of the *ustaša* movement [180 *pp. 84–6*].

The unfavourable conditions for resistance in Serbia proper (and the strength of German forces there) led the communist partisans to retreat into Bosnia in 1941. This was an extremely mixed area in ethnic terms. Here the wartime situation was marked by frequent inter-ethnic massacres; Serbian *četnici* and Croatian *ustaše* killed each other and the Muslims; Muslims were generally victims but one group (21,000 strong) was recruited into the German SS in 1943 and committed a number of massacres in northern and eastern Bosnia in the summer of 1944 [190 *pp. 189–91*]. The communist Partisans, in contrast, limited their activities to defending villages against attack from any side, reserving their main strength for the fight against the Nazis and those who collaborated with them. This policy brought dividends in the shape of support from all groups except the Albanians of Kosovo. There the Partisan struggle had to be abandoned, as the incorporation of Kosovo into Albania during the war was generally welcomed by the local population, who regarded Yugoslavia as an oppressive, Serb-run state [38 *p. 253*].

Macedonia, too, was a problematic area for the Yugoslav communists: most Macedonians welcomed the wartime annexation of the region by Bulgaria (until they saw what it meant) and in 1941 the local communist organization, under Metodi Shatarov, went over to the Bulgarian Communist Party. Tito expelled Shatarov from the Yugoslav party and made sure that future Macedonian communist leaders were pro-Yugoslav. In 1943 he sent Svetozar Vukmanović-Tempo to Macedonia to organize the Partisan movement. Tempo gained Macedonian support by promising that after the war Macedonian unity would be achieved by the inclusion in federal Yugoslavia of an autonomous Macedonia, which would cover Macedonian areas presently in Bulgaria and Greece as well. This commitment was not mentioned subsequently, but one of the resolutions issued by AVNOJ* (the Anti-Fascist Council of the People's Liberation of Yugoslavia) in November 1943 did include Macedonia in the list of federal Yugoslav republics [59 *pp. 215–16*].

It is harder to explain the third point, the reason for the independent position that communist Yugoslavia took up towards the Soviet Union and Stalin after the war. After all, there were many similarities between the Yugoslav communists and their counterparts elsewhere: the techniques employed to seize power, the goals of the movement and the ideology of Marxism-Leninism were all the same. It would not have been possible to predict Yugoslav communist independence before 1941 (and no one did). It was partly a result of the way the communists came to power, in and through war. In subsequent polemics the Yugoslavs always insisted that Soviet assistance had played no significant part in their wartime victory. There was some truth in this. But it is also true to say that victory was achieved in alliance with the Soviet Union. The German retreat from Yugoslavia in 1944, which made the victory of the Partisans a certainty, was enforced by Soviet attacks on German forces elsewhere. It was, moreover, impossible for Tito to prevent the Red Army from entering Yugoslavia after the war in pursuit of the retreating Germans. Hence there were Soviet military forces on the spot in 1945. These could have been used to impose a more pliant Yugoslav leadership, if Stalin had really wanted to. There had, after all, been plenty of signs during the war that Tito was far more inclined to independent action than the average communist leader. The Second Declaration of AVNOJ, issued at Jajce in November 1943 without consulting Stalin, was a particularly glaring example. It transformed that body into the future republican Yugoslav government [*Doc. 1*]. This was entirely at variance with Stalin's policy of alliance with the Western powers and coalition between existing governments in exile and resistance movements. 'The boss is furious' wrote Manuilsky, one of Stalin's leading international officials. 'He considers this a stab in the back of the Soviet Union' [180 *p. 12*]. But Stalin forgave even this. When Tito visited Moscow in September 1944 he was able to secure an agreement with the Soviet leader which provided for the subordination of the Red Army to local civilian control, and its withdrawal once victory was assured, and Stalin kept to this. It was, comments Mastny, 'the decision he had the strongest reason to regret' [45 *p. 73*].

During the first few years after the war the only apparent difference between Yugoslavia and the other People's Democracies was its greater radicalism. Communist Yugoslavia was 'the hard-boiled dictatorship' [185 *p. 81*]. It travelled the same road as its eastern neighbours, only more ruthlessly and more rapidly. In politics, the move to the one-party state was pretty well completed by November 1945: no candidate was allowed to stand for election against the Popular Front, and the Popular Front was entirely dominated by the communist party. The repression of political opponents, and acts of revenge against collaborators in 1945–46, were more ruthless than anywhere else, with the possible exception of Bulgaria. The secret police, or OZNA*, was as vicious as police forces in other communist countries. Its chief, Ranković, admitted in 1949 that 47 per cent of arrests carried out in 1945 had been unjustified. The trial of the Agrarian leader Dragoljub Jovanović in October 1947 was as much of a Stalinist show trial as simultaneous events in Bulgaria and Romania. There was a revealing conversation between Ranković and Tito on the subject: 'He must be arrested', said Tito. 'It will be hard to get anything on him', replied Ranković. 'Then make him guilty of something', was Tito's rejoinder [3 *p. 45*]. Jovanović was not the only one. Two other opposition leaders, Franjo Gazi of the Croat Peasant Party and Miloš Trifunović of the Serbian Radical Party were also sent to prison at this time. This was the tip of the iceberg. The repressions of 1945 to 1947 eventually made political life outside the communist party framework impossible – exactly as in the neighbouring states [187 *p. 177*].

The picture was the same in the economic sphere. A Five Year Plan of rapid industrialization, stressing heavy industry and a very high rate of investment (25 per cent per annum) was issued in 1947; this anticipated developments in the rest of Eastern Europe by two years. Eleven per cent of the country's agricultural land was expropriated from big landowners (40 per cent of it had belonged to ethnic Germans) and handed over to landless peasants and former communist Partisans [185 *p. 90*]. A system of compulsory grain deliveries was started straight away, 31 collective farms were set up in 1945 [51 *p. 178*], and the Five Year Plan envisaged that the proportion of state and collective farms would reach 50 per cent by 1952 [98 *p. 208*].

Yugoslavia's independent domestic policies disturbed Stalin; he was even more concerned by the tendency the Yugoslav communists displayed to set themselves up as a rival power centre in the Balkans. Yugoslavia undertook a number of foreign policy initiatives which were highly unwelcome to Stalin. The Yugoslav communists had long favoured the idea of a Balkan Federation, because it would unite Bulgaria and Yugoslavia and thereby solve the Macedonian problem. Moreover, a wider federation including Albania would deal with the problem of Kosovo as well. The Bulgarians did not like the idea of joining a federation, in which they would merely become the seventh Yugoslav republic. Stalin rejected this solution of Balkan problems as premature in 1945.

In 1947 the Yugoslavs again took up the federation idea, and this time the Bulgarians were more responsive. After negotiations with the Bulgarian leader Georgi Dimitrov, the Bled Agreements of July 1947 were signed, providing for close cooperation short of federation. They also provided for cultural contacts between Yugoslav Macedonia and the part of Macedonia that lay within Bulgaria, known as Pirin Macedonia [180 *p. 37*]. This was intended to be a first step towards union. In January 1948, Dimitrov commented publicly on plans for a federation, saying that 'the question must inevitably mature, though it is not on the agenda at present' [185 *p. 124*].

At this point Stalin intervened, calling Tito and Dimitrov to Moscow (Tito sent Kardelj and Djilas instead). A meeting was held between the four men on 10 February 1948, at which Stalin criticized Yugoslavia for deliberately keeping him in the dark about Balkan policies. The Bled Agreements, he said, had been made in defiance of his instructions to wait until a peace treaty had been signed with Bulgaria. Moreover, Yugoslavia had tried to secure a military base in Albania on the grounds that it was needed to protect that country against the threat of Greek intervention. This, said Stalin, was merely a pretext for expansionism. Moreover, Yugoslav support for the Greek communist uprising was likely to embroil him with the West. Stalin insisted that the rising must cease immediately, on the grounds that 'the most powerful state in the world, the United States' would never permit them 'to break its lines of communication in the Mediterranean' [2 *p. 178*].

Surprisingly, Stalin also supported the Yugoslav project of a Balkan federation. But he insisted that the treaty must be concluded immediately. This was clearly a provocation on Stalin's part, as was his suggestion that Yugoslavia should 'swallow Albania'.

On their return to Belgrade the Yugoslavs decided not to proceed with the federation, as they feared that Bulgaria would be a 'Soviet Trojan horse' within their country. In addition, various critical remarks were made about Stalin's policies at a meeting of the Central Committee (CC)* of the CPY, held on 1 March 1948. What Tito and his colleagues did not know was that these remarks were immediately reported to Stalin by Sreten Žujović, the most pro-Soviet member of the Yugoslav leadership, who saw it as his internationalist duty to tell Moscow everything. The Soviet leader's reply took the shape of the thunderbolt of 27 March 1948: an extremely hostile letter to the Yugoslav CC. This accused certain party leaders, namely Djilas and Ranković, of creating an 'anti-Soviet atmosphere' in Yugoslavia, and brought up a list of complaints about alleged deviations from Marxism, including the 'undemocratic character of the Yugoslav Communist Party', its failure to engage in the class struggle in town and country and the alleged fact that a British spy was employed in the Yugoslav Foreign Office [180 *p. 43*]. The Yugoslavs replied on 13 April, refuting all the accusations. Stalin, in his turn, sent an even fiercer missive on 4 May. The letter of 4 May repeated the earlier complaints and added others. It also invited the Yugoslav leaders to a meeting of the Cominform*, so that the issues could be discussed in an international forum.

But Tito and the other Yugoslav leaders refused to attend. One reason for the refusal was their realization that 'there was no guarantee that Tito would return alive from such a meeting' [185 *p. 134*]. Instead, they sent a letter proclaiming their fidelity to the doctrines of Marx, Engels, Lenin and Stalin and their determination to carry on constructing socialism while remaining loyal to the Soviet Union. Stalin was not convinced. When the Cominform met at Bucharest in June 1948 it passed a resolution excommunicating the CPY and inviting 'sound forces' within it to 'compel their present leaders to admit their mistakes openly and to correct them' or failing that to get rid of them [17 *p. 621*]. According to Khrushchev, Stalin told him: 'I will shake my little finger and there will be no more Tito. He will fall' [10 *p. 600*]. But it did not happen. Stalin overestimated the strength of support for his position among Yugoslav communists. There were only two party leaders who took his side, Žujović and Hebrang, and one army general, Arso Jovanović. In the party as a whole there were probably 50,000 'Cominformists' (supporters of the Cominform's anti-Tito resolution of June 1948). This would amount to 19.5 per cent of the membership in 1948. Of these, 16,000 were arrested and sentenced (including Žujović and Hebrang), and 8,000 were interned on the island concentration camp of Goli Otok.

Jovanović was shot while trying to escape across the border. Despite their relatively large numbers, the Cominformists were crushed with ease because they lacked a programme and failed to take the initiative. The failure of his supporters to overthrow Tito meant that Stalin had a choice between military invasion and acceptance of the situation. He eventually chose the latter option, though not without hesitation. In fact, he assembled an invasion force in Bulgaria in August 1949, but could not make up his mind to order it into action. Henceforth Yugoslavia was free to follow its own unique path [180 *pp. 149–51, 225–6*].

## THE DEFEATED SIDE

Once the communists had come to power in Eastern Europe the non-communists were the defeated side; no one paid much attention to them in subsequent years. Since 1989, the situation has changed greatly and there has been a revival of interest in the losers. Historians now spend much time uncovering evidence on resistance to communism and to specific communist policies, such as agricultural collectivization. The studies of Karel Kaplan on Czechoslovakia [120; 121; 123; 124], Krystyna Kersten on Poland [164], Denis Deletant on Romania [174], and Vladimir Migev on Bulgaria [110] deserve particular mention.

There was certainly plenty of local resistance to the communist takeover of power, despite the hopelessness of the effort. In Bulgaria, the fight against communism was conducted in 1947 by Nikola Petkov, the Agrarian leader, with almost foolhardy courage; instead of fleeing the country, he insisted on standing up in the Bulgarian parliament, the Grand National Assembly, denouncing the communists for incompetence and arrogance, and accusing them of a level of repression that outdid the Fascists. He called for the complete restoration of civil liberty in Bulgaria. This defiance was punished by judicial murder. He was sentenced to death for 'organizing an armed plot' and executed soon afterwards (in September 1947) [107 *p. 189*]. Petkov's fate had the effect of cowing the Bulgarian opposition. In the early 1950s, however, spontaneous resistance to agricultural collectivization broke out; it was crushed by the sending of thousands of peasants to labour camps (a total of 110,000 suffered this fate between 1946 and 1956) [110 *p. 71*].

In Czechoslovakia, resistance was made more difficult by the consensus politics of the post-1945 period; the communists were able to claim that their opponents were reactionaries who opposed the will of the vast majority of the people, as expressed in free elections. In the Czech lands, the communist party received 40 per cent of the vote at the May 1946 elections. In Slovakia, however, they did not do so well, receiving 30 per cent, while their opponents, the Slovak Democrats, gained 62 per cent. An attempt made by the communists to remove them from the coalition government in November

1947 failed because of the opposition of their non-communist colleagues in the National Front. A compromise was worked out by which the Communist Party of Slovakia received five cabinet posts, but the Democrats kept their seven seats. The Slovak communists were very disappointed: 'We are the last state in the East where those who stand against the Soviet Union have still not been removed. ... Our weak point is the weak force at our disposal' [123 *p. 103*]. In the long run this made no difference, as the definitive decision was made three months later, in Prague rather than Bratislava.

This time there was less resistance: the demonstrative mass resignation of the non-communist ministers on 20 February 1948 in protest against the refusal of the communist Minister of the Interior, Václav Nosek, to dismiss eight communist district police chiefs he had just appointed, was sabotaged by the refusal of the Social Democrats to resign from the cabinet. In any case, the whole procedure placed far too great a burden on the frail shoulders of President Beneš, who was, it seems, expected to carry out the resistance to communism single-handed by refusing to appoint replacements for those ministers who had resigned. When the communists called a general strike, on 24 February 1948, as a means of pressurizing the Czechoslovak President to accept the resignations, the National Socialists, who had started off the crisis, found themselves unable to oppose this popular protest. They issued a declaration allowing members of their party to participate in it [116 *p. 189*]. Their leader, Hubert Ripka, had already surrendered. He wrote to Gottwald on 23 February, saying that 'as a politician' he realized he had lost the battle, and would now 'retire into private life' [38 *p. 422*].

# CHAPTER THREE

# THE IMPOSITION OF THE STALINIST SYSTEM

## THE PHASE OF RECONSTRUCTION

Postwar communist policies in Eastern Europe evolved through two stages. First, between 1945 and 1947, they were 'moderate' and the main aim was postwar reconstruction. Then, in 1948, they became 'socialist' and were directed towards a planned economy and social transformation. The policies pursued after 1948 were very largely imitative of the Soviet model. This stage lasted until Stalin's death in 1953. Sometimes the second stage is in turn subdivided into two periods, before and after 1949, with much justification, since imitation of the Soviet model was far more pronounced after that date [28; 56]. Nevertheless, we shall stick to two stages here, for the sake of simplicity.

In analysing the question of communist policy in the immediate postwar period, two distinctions need to be made: between politics and economics, and between former allied and former enemy countries. In politics, the period of 'moderation' between 1945 and 1947 meant the continuation of a coalition government with a definite role for the non-communist parties. This is clearest in Czechoslovakia and Hungary, though, formally speaking, coalition governments existed everywhere. As the leader of the Communist Party of Czechoslovakia, Klement Gottwald, said in April 1945: 'The immediate target is not Soviets and socialism but the really consistent working out of the democratic and national revolution' [130 *p. 360*]. A year later the line was still the same. Georgi Dimitrov proclaimed that 'the immediate task is neither the realization of socialism nor the introduction of the Soviet system but the consolidation of a truly democratic and parliamentarian system' [37 *p. 134*].

It should be added that the existence of coalition governments and the possibility of free political competition, including freely held elections, was not regarded as a permanent option by the communists. The threat of force was held in reserve. Sometimes it was brandished quite openly, even at this early stage. Gottwald told the members of his party in 1946 that 'if the election results are unsatisfactory', which was improbable, 'our party, and the workers, will even then continue to have within their grasp sufficient means, weapons and methods to correct the results of merely mechanical voting in which reactionary and subversive elements have been victorious' [36 *p. 17*].

In economics, communist moderation initially implied holding off on state control of industry so as not to break up broad alliances. The manifesto drawn up by the Czechoslovak communist leaders during the war, and put forward as an agreed programme in April 1945 in the small town of Košice in Slovakia, was a moderate document which did not include the nationalization of industry [*Doc. 5*]. It was the Social Democrats and President Beneš who insisted on adding a reference to nationalization. The Czechoslovak President then asked Gottwald to prepare a decree on the nationalization of industry. This decree was worked out jointly by the communists and the Social Democrats. It covered 60 per cent of industrial output, but met with no opposition from the other coalition parties [123 *p. 35*].

The first step taken by the postwar coalition governments in Eastern Europe was usually to nationalize (in other words to confiscate) the property of Germans and collaborators. This was not controversial; and no one seems to have imagined the possibility that the confiscated property could be sold off to private entrepreneurs. The confiscations were followed over the next two years by general laws of nationalization. These had raised the proportion of industry under state control to 80 per cent in Poland and in Czechoslovakia by 1947. Very little opposition was met with from the former owners of industrial enterprises, for several reasons. It was common ground all over Europe at this time that the future belonged to either state-run industry or a mixed system. In prewar Poland the state had had an important stake in industry, while during the war the Nazis had destroyed the Polish business classes by taking over most of their factories. In June 1946, the leading opponent of the communists, Stanisław Mikołajczyk, did not feel able to ask his supporters to oppose nationalization in a referendum on the issue. Where there were objections from the Right, they were partly overcome by mass action. The communists paid lip-service to the idea of workers' control, which was a powerful rallying cry in 1945. Włodzimierz Brus comments: 'Workers' self-management or control was used in Eastern Europe as a tool of nationalization and was quickly suppressed soon afterwards' [81 *p. 599*]. In Poland the 'left turn' of October 1944 meant that the workers were encouraged to set up Factory Councils, which directly took over the factories. After May 1945 Gomułka 'turned back to the right'. He launched a campaign to reduce the power of the Factory Councils. Some workers were jailed for going on strike against this new line [171 *pp. 520–3*].

There was a similar shift of policy in Czechoslovakia. Factory Councils developed spontaneously in May 1945. This was a movement independent of the communist party, and independent of the communist-run trade union federation, the ROH*. The communists could not tolerate this situation. In June 1945 they denounced the Factory Councils as 'syndicalist', and they set up a rival system based on local trade union cells and a dues-paying membership. In October 1945 the Decree on Factory Councils was issued. This gave the ROH absolute control over elections to the Factory Councils; the workers had no choice of candidates because the ROH put forward a single slate, and no other group was allowed to present itself for election. Moreover, the Factory Councils themselves were emasculated: the decree of October 1945 made the running of the enterprise 'the concern of the managing staff alone'. It also provided that 'the Factory Councils shall not have the right to interfere with the management and operation of the enterprise'. Unsurprisingly, the Factory Council elections of spring 1947 were a farce, marked by passivity and abstention on the part of the workers. In the context of the Prague coup of February 1948 the Factory Councils were then brought back to life, but on a temporary and strictly subordinate basis. In March 1948 they were in effect abolished by being merged with the local trade union branches [114 *pp. 170–3*; 126 *p. 267*]. In East Germany too the communists were completely opposed to independent initiatives. As soon as Ulbricht arrived from Moscow (in May 1945) he gave orders that the leftist 'liberation committees' that had sprung up should be wound up, as they were, he alleged, 'a cover organization for the Nazis' [12 *p. 318*]. Nationalization in East Germany was organized exclusively from the top down. Even so, Factory Councils did emerge there. They resisted the introduction of piecework wages and other non-egalitarian measures, so that by April 1948 the proportion of East German workers on piecework was down to 20 per cent [135 *p. 27*]. They also played a part in resisting 'socialist emulation' campaigns. Eventually, in 1948, the authorities ordered their suppression [140 *p. 113*].

In the former enemy countries of Bulgaria, Hungary and Romania, where there was little German property to confiscate, moves to create state-owned industry were very gradual. In Romania the state share of the economy as late as 1947 was 11 per cent and in Bulgaria 16 per cent. In Hungary in November 1946 it was 45 per cent [80 *pp. 600–6*]. Nationalization was delayed here for two reasons: the peace treaties had not yet been signed, the needs of reconstruction were paramount and it was important not to scare off private enterprise. A senior Hungarian communist, József Révai, told a congress of coal miners in May 1945: 'The capitalists' profit is a price worth paying for their participation in the country's economic revival.' István Kossa, the communist General Secretary of the Hungarian Trades Union Congress, stressed in the same month that 'the party's political line is the recognition of private property' [150 *pp. 170–3*]. (The coal mines were, however, nationalized in December.) Similar comments were made in Bulgaria. The communist Minister of the Interior, Anton Yugov, stated in

September 1944 that 'there is no truth in the rumour that the government intends to nationalize private enterprise' (although it was somewhat disingenuous of him to disavow 'any intention of establishing a communist regime' in Bulgaria). The head of the Supreme Economic Council, Dobri Terpeshev, used similar language: 'Private initiative will not be handicapped but supported' [37 *p. 134*].

It was not surprising, in this context, that the initial steps in postwar economic planning were dominated by goals of reconstruction and a recovery from the miserable standard of living the population had endured during the Second World War. All the economic plans announced for the three years between 1947 and 1949 had modest targets of recovery to slightly above the prewar level of output. In Hungary they expected to exceed this by 1 per cent by 1949; in Czechoslovakia by 10 per cent; in Poland by 16 per cent; in Bulgaria by 44 per cent. Only in Yugoslavia, exceptional as ever, was anything more ambitious attempted: the prewar level was to be outstripped by 93 per cent.

The moderation of 1945 to 1947 also implied a rejection of agricultural collectivization. The devastating consequences of the introduction of collective farms (*kolkhozy\**) in the Soviet Union were known to the peasants of Eastern Europe, or at least to their political representatives, such as, in Poland, the SL (Peasants' Party). Fear of collectivization was the reason given by the SL for refusing to enter into alliance with the communists in 1943 [159 *p. 385*]. But, as Gomułka pointed out in his reply, the communists themselves opposed the idea of collectivization. The Hungarian communists were still publicly opposing collectivization as late as 1947 [143 *p. 246*]. What was on the agrarian agenda was not collectivization but land reform, in other words the abolition of large-scale landownership. It must be added, however, that where large landed estates existed before 1945 they were not all divided among poor and landless peasants after confiscation. Part of the land was retained by the state. In East Germany, for instance, 35 per cent of agricultural land was confiscated in 1945; but one-third of this remained in the hands of state and local authorities. The view was strongly held that small-scale peasant agriculture was unproductive, so for the communists the land reforms of 1945 were only a temporary solution.

Communist moderation between 1945 and 1947 clearly needed an ideological justification as well. This was provided by the veteran Bulgarian communist Dimitrov. In February 1946 he stressed that the Soviet example of proletarian dictatorship was not compulsory: 'Not every party will follow the same road to socialism. They will not follow the Soviet model exactly but each will act in their own way' [57 *p. 249*]. The countries of Eastern Europe, all communist spokesmen agreed, were currently in a situation of 'People's Democracy'. This was distinguished very clearly from the dictatorship of the proletariat by Gomułka in November 1946: 'Polish People's

Democracy is not a dictatorship of the proletariat and Poland will attain socialism without such a dictatorship. Our democracy is not to be compared with Soviet democracy' [159 p. 203].

## THE TURNING-POINT OF 1947

There were several indications in 1947 that Eastern Europe was passing from stage one to stage two (from 'moderation' to 'socialism'). There was nothing permanent about the phase of moderate policies; it was understood to be a period of transition. As Miklos Molnár has put it: 'the formula for a pluralist people's democracy was not an alternative' but 'the springboard from which the party prepared to make the great leap into the Stalin system' [153 p. 135]. The Czechoslovak communist leader Klement Gottwald was perhaps boasting when he said in 1949: 'We prepared for (the coup of) February 1948 from 1945 onwards, and particularly from 1947' [123 p. 105]. But the question at issue was not the fact of transition, but how long the process would take. The Hungarian communist leader Rákosi said in 1945 that the socialist transformation will be preceded by a 'transitional phase which might last a decade or more' [29 p. 50]. As it turned out, this was an overestimate. The end of the 'moderate' phase occurred in the context of the threatening international developments known as the 'coming of the Cold War'.

The most important diplomatic turning-point in this process was Stalin's refusal to allow any of the Eastern European governments to attend the July 1947 Paris Conference that was called to discuss the Marshall Plan. The Czechoslovak government had initially voted unanimously in favour of attending (4 July 1947). In other words, the communists had also supported the idea. But a few days later a Czechoslovak delegation was summoned to Moscow to discuss this question. Stalin not only explained his objections to the plan; he also in effect forbade the Czechoslovaks to attend. They naturally complied [*Doc. 12*]. There were both political and economic reasons for the Soviet attitude. In the field of international trade, the USSR's Eastern European position declined continuously from 1946 onwards. Here are some figures for the proportion of imports that came from the USSR:

|  | 1945 | 1946 | 1947 |
|---|---|---|---|
| Bulgaria | 80% | 82% | 60% |
| Czechoslovakia | 33% | 13% | 7% |
| Hungary | 26% | 79% | 11% |
| Poland | 91% | 69% | 25% |

*Source:* [80 p. 582].

Political intervention was needed to reverse this trend; the Marshall Plan would have only strengthened it.

Let us now look at the domestic situation. The 'mixed economy' introduced by the partial nationalization measures of 1945 was inherently unstable. The private and state sectors entered into competition. The state took sides in this contest, fearing a victory of the private sector. State ownership of industry grew gradually but inexorably. In Hungary, the proportion of workers in the state sector grew from 22 per cent in the summer of 1946 to 45 per cent in November 1946 and 60 per cent in December 1947. In March 1948 all factories employing over 100 workers were nationalized; the threshold was lowered to ten workers in December 1949, thus completing the process. Similar figures could be quoted for the rest of Eastern Europe, with Albania, Yugoslavia, Poland and Czechoslovakia moving more quickly, Romania and Bulgaria starting late but also moving quickly to complete state control by 1948, and East Germany bringing up the rear (because Stalin was not prepared until 1952 to close off the option of German unity by altering the economic structure of his zone of occupation).

Full-scale nationalization made it possible for the governments to engage in more directive economic planning. In this field, at first sight rather arcane, but in fact central to the development of the whole society, conflicts developed in 1947–48 between rival government bodies with responsibility for planning. The Social Democrats, often entrenched in the existing planning offices, favoured balanced economic planning and the use of Western credits to pay for the import of machinery; the Communists favoured rapid growth in close alliance with the Soviet Union and using Soviet methods. The decision of July 1947 to reject the Marshall Plan was one nail in the coffin of Social Democratic planning. The move to a political monopoly for the communist party was another. The contest ended everywhere in 1948 with the defeat of the Social Democratic planners and the abandonment of balanced economic planning in favour of voluntaristic extremes. In Poland the communist planning victory came in February 1948: the plan prepared in 1946 by the Central Planning Office, under a team of PPS* economists led by Czesław Bobrowski, was scrapped and a new plan prepared by the State Economic Planning Commission, led by Hilary Minc, the economics specialist of the communist leadership [158]. In Czechoslovakia in October 1947 the communists and Social Democrats put forward rival plans. The difference between them was that the communists called for a higher overall rate of growth, a quarter more investment and a much greater stress on heavy industry. The debate between the two positions continued until the communist seizure of power in February 1948. After that they were able to purge the Central Planning Commission of moderate planners. Similar events took place in Hungary, where there was a conflict between three different planning offices, owing allegiance to three different political parties, the Smallholders, the Social Democrats and the Communists. Eventually the communist-controlled Supreme Economic Council was victorious [80 *pp. 610–17*].

Politically, the move from moderation to full communist control implied the liquidation, or at least the subordination, of the other parties. With regard to the Social Democrats, the chosen method, in every case, was absorption into the communist party. This can easily be explained. The communists' view was that all political parties represented social classes; there could therefore only be room for one working-class party, although to the extent that the bourgeoisie and the peasantry survived their parties could also be allowed to continue. Even so, there was some doubt about the future of Social Democracy at first. Absorption followed the achievement of sole power rather than preceding it in every case except those of Slovakia, where the Social Democrats and Communists merged in September 1944 in the context of an armed uprising which they hoped would bring them to power (it did not, as it was put down by German troops) and East Germany, where the impulse behind the communist decision to swallow up the SPD was the fear of an electoral débâcle. The news of the disastrous failure of the communist party at the Austrian elections of November 1945 (they gained four out of a total of 165 seats) led the Soviet occupying authorities to press for the speediest possible unification of the two parties [138 *p. 276*]. In April 1946 the KPD and the East German SPD* joined together to form the SED (Socialist Unity Party of Germany). This hasty merger was followed by a systematic purge of the membership of the new party over the next few years.

The reason for delaying until 1948 in other cases was probably the need to purify the existing Social Democratic parties of right-wingers before the merger took place. The initial starting-point everywhere was the existence of a factional division within the Social Democratic parties of Eastern Europe over two issues: cooperation with the communists and the level of radicalism in social policy. Usually these two coincided: those who favoured close cooperation with the communists were also left-wingers (there were minor exceptions to this rule, such as Bohumír Laušman in Czechoslovakia, a left-winger who wanted to preserve the independence of his party). Outright opponents of the communists, in contrast, were removed fairly soon after 1945. Between 1945 and 1948 Social Democratic parties generally consisted of a 'left' which wanted a merger with the communists, and a 'centre' which opposed this. The period between 1947 and 1948 saw the expulsion of the latter, which was an essential preliminary step to a complete merger. Thus the centrists were expelled from Hungarian Social Democracy in February 1948; and the leader of centrism in Poland, Cyrankiewicz, saw which way the wind was blowing in March 1948 when he visited Moscow. On his return he began to support the line of a merger. In Czechoslovakia the 'left'

Social Democrats had to be restrained from joining the CPCz as individuals after February 1948. Gottwald told their leader, Zdeněk Fierlinger, that his job was to stay in the party and devote his efforts to building it up. What Fierlinger did not know was that the CPCz leaders had already decided to absorb his party [120 *p. 162*]. The merger eventually took place in June 1948.

Sharp measures were taken against rebellious Social Democrats in Bulgaria and Romania. Kosta Lulchev, leader of Bulgarian Social Democracy, was arrested and given a fifteen-year jail sentence in July 1948; this allowed the faction led by Dimitur Neikov to take over the party and lead it into a merger with the communists at the end of 1948. In Romania, a split in the Socialist Party took place in March 1946, with the pro-communist wing agreeing to go forward to the elections with a joint list alongside the communists. In October 1947 it resolved to merge with the communists; the first congress of the merged party was held in February 1948, under the name Romanian Workers' Party. The anti-communist faction, under Titel Petrescu, organized an Independent Socialist Party, but it was dissolved by the authorities in 1948 and Petrescu himself was arrested for illegally distributing leaflets.

The moves towards full state control of the economy, the definitive Soviet break with the West, and the crushing or absorption of the communists' political rivals, largely completed by 1948, marked the transition from the 'moderate' to the 'Stalinist' stage in Eastern Europe, which lasted until 1953. In the next chapter we shall examine the predominant features and trends of development in this next stage of Eastern European communist history.

# CHAPTER FOUR

# STALIN'S SYSTEM AT ITS HEIGHT

It is generally recognized that the period between 1948 and 1953 was one of maximum uniformity in Eastern Europe, at least as a goal. Yugoslavia, which broke with Stalin in 1948, is the exception; but as it remained a communist country, and made few changes in domestic policy in the early years, many of the features mentioned apply there too until at least 1950. In this section we shall adopt a comparative approach, indicating the main characteristics of Stalinism and showing how they applied in Eastern Europe. It will be helpful to subdivide the topic into politics, the economy, society and culture.

## THE POLITICS OF STALINISM IN EASTERN EUROPE

After 1948 every country in Eastern Europe was run by a single party, which had a monopoly of power and claimed to rule in the name of the working class. In most cases communist parties renamed themselves 'workers' parties' after absorbing the previous Social Democratic or Socialist parties. We have already examined this important and universal phenomenon. Other (non-working-class) parties still existed but in a strictly subordinate role under the aegis of National Front or Popular Front 'coalitions'. Needless to say, communist party rule did not mean the rule of ordinary party members; it meant the rule of a narrow oligarchy, either the Politbureau of the party's Central Committee (CC), or the Secretariat of the party's Central Committee, or a combination of the two (there was often interlocking membership). Moreover, one of the characteristics of East European Stalinism was that Stalin had his local counterparts, the leaders of the separate national parties, with the result that until 1953 oligarchical rule was replaced by individual control. In Hungary, for instance, the 'cult of personality' reached such preposterous heights under Rákosi that every mention of his name received a storm of applause in any meeting. 'When we say Rákosi', proclaimed his second-in-command Ernő Gerő, 'we mean the Hungarian people. And when we say the Hungarian people we mean Rákosi' [150 *p. 236*].

## ECONOMIC OBJECTIVES AND SOCIAL CHANGES

In the economy the aim was complete state control of economic life, and planned economic growth on the Soviet model. This implied squeezing out the remnants of capitalism, in town and country. This was much easier in the towns. The remains of private enterprise disappeared from industry. Retail trade passed out of the hands of independent shopkeepers. In agriculture, collectivization on the Soviet model was the ideal to be aimed at. Collectivization was seen not as a strengthening of the existing agricultural co-operatives but their destruction, even though the official title for collective farms was usually 'agricultural producers' cooperatives' or some similar expression. The communists' aim was to achieve the 'higher level' collective in which farms would be owned in common and the income of the individual collective farmer would be determined entirely by the amount of labour contributed. Whether this was conducive to maximum economic efficiency was less important at this epoch than its social effects. Full collectivization would mean the conclusive liquidation of capitalism, and of the rural capitalist class, the 'kulaks' (the Russian term was often used, though not in Poland).

In practice the move towards collective farms was 'more cautious and sophisticated' than it had been in the Soviet Union [81 *p. 10*]. Initially the associations set up were of the loosest type, analogous to the TOZy* (Associations for the Joint Cultivation of the Land) which had been established in the Soviet Union in the 1920s. Under this system the peasants continued to own their land, and even kept their animals. These were really agricultural producers' associations. But during the early 1950s they were gradually replaced by genuine collective farms. In Czechoslovakia, the share of the 'lowest form' (in other words the loosest form) of JZD* (Unified Agricultural Cooperative) fell from 96.1 per cent of the total in 1949 to 15.7 per cent in 1952. In 1954 the loosest cooperatives were entirely abolished, leaving only the higher forms, in which land, animals and implements all belonged to the collective [61 *p. 61*]. Various measures were used to force the peasants into the collective farms. Prosperous farmers ('kulaks') could be penalized with high tax burdens and high delivery quotas; in Hungary they could also be placed on special 'kulak lists' and subjected to harassment. Eventually, if they proved obstinate, their property was confiscated and they were sent to prison camps.

The move to collectivization accelerated after 1948, to reach full speed in 1951. Then resistance set in. A partial retreat was already visible in 1952: there is evidence that even during Stalin's lifetime some governments were responsive to the pressure of popular discontent or evident defects in the systems adopted. In Romania, a decree was issued in September 1951 providing for the establishment of agricultural producers' cooperatives, along-

side the collective farms. In these new cooperatives the peasants could retain
their land; by October 1952 there were as many producers' cooperatives as
collective farms [59 *p. 502*]. In Yugoslavia, perhaps coincidentally, peasant
resistance to collectivization also led to retreat in 1951. Between 1949 and
1951 the CPY had pushed forward collectivization very rapidly, wishing to
prove that the Cominform's accusations of failure in this respect were
unfounded. Very high rates of collectivization were achieved in some republics
(61 per cent in Macedonia, 45 per cent in Montenegro) [180 *pp. 135–6*]. But
in November 1951 it was announced that in future the main stress would be
on 'general agricultural co-operatives' not collective farms [195 *p. 73*]. In
Bulgaria, the rate of collectivization, hectic in 1950 (the proportion of arable
land collectivized rose from 11 per cent to 41 per cent between May and
October) slowed practically to a standstill in 1952 in response to the peasant
revolts of 1951 [110].

With the economy largely under state control it became possible to
engage in systematic, planned economic development of the Stalinist type.
Five Year Plans, copied from the Soviet model of the 1930s, began to be
implemented in Eastern Europe at various dates after 1948. The planning
process was often preceded, as we saw earlier, by conflicts between rival
planners and rival plans. The communists, now in sole power, inevitably got
their way in these battles. State Planning Offices were now set up. They were
copies of similar institutions which had existed in the Soviet Union since the
1930s. The Five Year Plans drawn up by these offices, although already
biased towards securing the fastest possible growth of heavy industry, were
then made even more ambitious in response to the outbreak of the Korean
War (1950).

The military requirements of the Korean War led Moscow to put pressure on its East European allies to increase armaments production and raise
targets for industrial production. They were told at the end of 1950 to get
ready for a possible invasion by the United States [121 *p. 118*]. But they
were also told that the Soviet Union might take the offensive in Europe to
take the pressure off the Chinese, who were not doing very well in Korea at
that point [119 *pp. 165–6*]. The target for the increase in the Net Material
Product (a measure which was the Eastern bloc's equivalent of the West's
Gross Domestic Product, except that services and depreciation were excluded) was raised from 148 to 170 in Czechoslovakia, 163 to 230 in Hungary,
and 180 to 212 in Poland [81 *pp. 19–20*].

There was also direct economic exploitation of the Eastern European
economies at this time, to the advantage of the Soviet Union. In Poland there
were compulsory deliveries of 'reparation coal' at specially low prices. Under
the agreement of August 1945 Poland had to send 8 million tons of coal
eastwards every year at $1.25 a ton, at a time when Denmark was offering
$12 a ton for this commodity. By 1948 the price gap had lessened (the

market price was $18, the USSR paid $14), but an increased quantity was demanded. In East Germany, the Soviet Occupation Zone (SBZ)*, a large number of factories were dismantled and transported eastwards in payment of war reparations. Soviet interests were also served by the 'mixed companies' set up there, and in Romania, Bulgaria and Hungary after the war. These continued to exist until 1954 [78 *p. 59*].

To secure rapid economic growth it was not sufficient to draw up plans and direct resources to the appropriate places. Changes in attitude to time and productivity were also needed, especially as many of the new industrial workers had an agrarian background. Patrick Kenney has examined this process in the Polish context [163]. Elemér Hankiss has enumerated the many communist party campaigns aimed at achieving greater productivity and a more effective use of time [146 *pp. 14–17*]. One method adopted was 'socialist emulation' between work brigades. Groups of workers would pledge to fulfil the plan ahead of schedule, as in Romania, where 'workers of many enterprises pledged to carry out the 1950 production programme by 21 December 1949 in honour of the 70th. birthday of Comrade Stalin' [4 *21 October 1949*].

Another, more effective, form of pressure on the labour force was 'Stakhanovism', in other words the encouragement of outstanding individual workers, whose productivity achievements were trumpeted in the local, national and international communist press. Each country had its own Stakhanov, on the Soviet model of the 1930s. In Poland in June 1948, the miner Vincenty Pstrowski was the 'first to break the output target by 260 per cent. ... His challenge was enthusiastically accepted' [4 *1 July 1948*]. In East Germany, the miner Adolf Hennecke mined 387 per cent of his normal quota during one shift in October 1948, setting off a movement of emulation which spread to every other industrial sector [135 *p. 32*]. The Hungarians, not to be outdone, invented the particularly absurd Ten or Five Minutes' Movement (whereby people arrived ten or five minutes early for work so as to get the machine ready for an immediate start) [146 *p. 16*]. The introduction of piece rates and the raising of output norms was a logical consequence of this approach. 'The norm was not something permanent', wrote the Bulgarian dissident Georgi Markov. 'As soon as it was overfulfilled by ten per cent that was the signal to raise it. In this way the stronger and more skilful workers annihilated the weaker and clumsier ones' [109 *p. 25*]. Hungary can serve as an example: in July 1949 output norms were raised on the basis of 1948's performance; in late 1950 they were raised on the basis of the spring 1950 performance. In June 1952 they were raised again. Moreover, overtime was worked but overtime wages were not paid (this was a Polish grievance that came to the surface in 1956) [23 *p. 249*]. Ordinary workers resisted as far as possible. That, however, is so far an untold story.

Social changes fall under two headings: deliberately induced modifications of the social structure and indirect by-products of economic processes. Stalinism was self-consciously 'proletarian'. The old middle classes had no place in this scheme of things, still less the aristocracy. The aristocracy had been removed in the first wave of land reform after 1945. Now the bourgeois were to be either driven out altogether (many did leave after 1948) or reduced to the proletarian level. The abolition of private ownership (including private house-ownership) naturally helped in this process. In addition, direct measures were taken, such as the '77,000 for industry' campaign in Czechoslovakia, which put its victims to work in factories [121 *p. 82*]. In Hungary, between 350,000 and 400,000 formerly middle-class families were forced to find a new place in society between 1945 and 1953 [72 *p. 317*]. The image the communists wanted to convey was that of a state of workers and peasants in which the workers either rose to the top or, if they remained at the factory bench, enjoyed improved standards. For the majority of the workers in the Stalinist period the reality was otherwise. The economic growth of the early 1950s was secured at their expense. The figures for real wages are eloquent on this point. Taking the level in 1950 as 100, wages had fallen in Czechoslovakia to 95 by 1953, to 85 in Hungary, and to 92 in Poland (this does not apply to Romania and East Germany, where they rose, by 10 per cent and 77 per cent respectively) [81 *p. 34*].

A minority of workers rose up the social scale. Since the state now had a much larger role to play, the state apparatus expanded immensely – between 1948 and 1954 it grew by 80 per cent in Hungary – and people had to be found to staff it [150 *p. 262*]. Former workers found a place in this expanding bureaucracy in the 1950s (in Hungary 227,000 of them [150 *p. 248*], in Czechoslovakia 250,000 [36 *p. 64*]). However, once ensconced in office they simply entered the 'new class' analysed by Milovan Djilas at the time. Djilas showed how in Yugoslavia the new bureaucrats had become marked off from the rest of society by power and privilege [68 *pp. 39–42*]. The situation was no different elsewhere in Eastern Europe. The topmost stratum of this class later came to be known by the name *nomenklatura*. This was the upper class of communist society. In Czechoslovakia, for instance, it comprised about 15,000 people in total [127 *p. 159*]. The public use of the term *nomenklatura* dates from the 1970s, but the phenomenon itself existed long before. The word simply meant a list of posts which could not be filled without the prior approval of the communist party; soon it came to be applied to the people who occupied those posts.

There were also indirect social changes. Both industrialization and collectivization had the effect of reducing the proportion of workers in agriculture and increasing those in industry, and raising the urban proportion of the nation. In the 1930s most East European countries were composed overwhelmingly of country-dwellers (the proportions were, in Albania, 88 per cent; in Bulgaria, 79 per cent; in Romania, 80 per cent; in Yugoslavia, 78 per cent; in Poland, 73 per cent). Proportions were lower in Czechoslovakia (52 per cent), Hungary (64 per cent) and East Germany (29 per cent) [79 *p. 83*]. By 1960 the respective figures had fallen to Romania 68 per cent rural, Bulgaria 62 per cent, Poland 52 per cent, Hungary 58 per cent, Czechoslovakia 43 per cent and East Germany 28 per cent [72 *pp. 281, 372*]. The result of the changes of the 1940s and 1950s was to convert many peasants into workers (in Poland in the 1960s over half the workers in industry had been brought up in the countryside) and many peasants' sons and daughters into members of the socialist bureaucracy. Former peasants and their children had reason to be grateful to the communist regimes, and this was a source of stability, at least in the early years.

## THE TEXTURE OF LIFE AND THOUGHT

The Stalinist system aimed to subordinate society to the state, and to create as homogeneous and uniform a society as possible. This at least was the ideal, and some attempt was made to achieve it. Alternative social organizations were treated with suspicion. Sometimes they were suppressed (as in the case of the scouts and the Catholic Youth Movement in Poland, and the People's College movement in Hungary); sometimes they were absorbed and neutralized. The churches were naturally an obstacle to this process of homogenization. Complete suppression was not attempted, except in the case of the Uniate Church in Romania, which was merged with the Orthodox Church, as had happened in the Soviet Union. In general, the Orthodox Church, because of its traditional political quietism, and its lack of a point of reference outside the country, was easily converted into an instrument of the regime (Patriarch Justinian Marina in Romania and Exarch Mihail in Bulgaria did as they were told) [59 *pp. 550–6*]. The Roman Catholics, with their allegiance to the Pope in Rome, were more of a problem. Various methods were used to bring them to heel. Leading churchmen were put on trial (the following received prison sentences: in Yugoslavia the Primate, Archbishop Aloysiye Stepinac; in Romania the Bishop of Timişoara, Augustin Pacha; in Albania the Metropolitan Archbishop of Dürres, Monseigneur Premushi; in Czechoslovakia Archbishop Beran; in Hungary both Cardinal Mindszenty and his successor, after show trials).

Poland, though, was an exception. Admittedly, there was plenty of friction between state and church. In July 1949 the Vatican excommunicated Catholics who supported the communist party. The regime replied with a law prescribing a prison sentence of up to five years for anyone who refused the sacraments to citizens for political reasons. By January 1950 over 500 priests, nuns and monks had been arrested on various pretexts. In March

1950 all church estates larger than 250 acres in area were expropriated; priests and bishops were to be supported from the income received from them. The Roman Catholic welfare organization *Caritas* was taken over by the authorities. But in other areas the state proceeded with caution. The Catholic University of Lublin continued to exist, and all the monasteries and seminaries in the country continued functioning. In any case, an agreement was soon reached with the Polish bishops (April 1950) which maintained unrestricted religious education in the schools and guaranteed autonomy to the Church in the religious sphere, in return for recognition of the regime and the bishops' signature on the Stockholm Peace Appeal, which was a Cold War propaganda campaign against the West by which Stalin set great store [159 *p. 248*]. It seemed that Poland might avoid the religious confrontations that had taken place elsewhere. But it was not to be. State pressure on the Church grew again in 1952 and 1953. In February 1953 the government took powers to veto all Church appointments, and forced all priests and bishops to take an oath of loyalty to the Polish People's Republic. In September 1953 Bishop Czesław Kaczmarek of Kielce was given a twelve-year sentence for allegedly spying for the United States and helping Ukrainian insurgents. The Primate, Cardinal Wyszyński, was confined to a monastery for failing to condemn him [159 *p. 251*; 170 *p. 18*].

Another means of pressure on the Churches was the promotion of rival religious movements, the members of which were often put in charge of vacant dioceses. In Poland, the clergy were encouraged to join the movement of 'Patriotic Priests'; but the lay believers were not forgotten either. For them the regime financed *Pax*, the Catholic Social Movement set up by the ex-Fascist Bolesław Piasecki, who had now changed sides. *Pax* aimed to reconcile communism with Catholicism; most believers regarded the organization with distaste. In Czechoslovakia, there was 'Catholic Action'; in Hungary, there was a 'Peace Movement for Catholic Priests'; but the most spectacular measure was taken in Romania, where the government tried to create a schismatic church, based on a 'Catholic Action Committee' led by the excommunicated priest Andreas Agota (March 1951) [59 *pp. 561–2*; 92 *pp. 264–85*].

Social questions naturally shade into cultural and intellectual matters. In these spheres, an attempt was made to impose a uniform system of 'Marxism-Leninism' and stamp out divergent views. The party regarded the transformation of culture as very important [179 *p. 40*]. The ultimate aim of the cultural campaigns of this period was to stamp out traditional culture and replace it with 'communist culture'. The doctrine of 'socialist realism' was imposed everywhere after 1948. The official definition, first proclaimed in 1934 in Moscow, and still authoritative fifteen years later, was that 'it requires from the artist a truthful, historically concrete representation of reality in its revolutionary development, combined with the task of ideological transformation and the education of the workers in the spirit of socialism'. This did not give very clear guidance, but it certainly implied a rejection of literary and artistic experimentation. It also implied vilifying the capitalist past (and the capitalist West) and painting the socialist present in bright, rosy colours. As the Hungarian Minister of Culture, József Révai, said in 1951, 'what the Party demands of our writers is that they present positive heroes to the people' [34 *p. 412*]. Socialist realism was an uncomfortable cultural strait-jacket for the intellectuals of Eastern Europe. It enforced 'a reversion to the techniques of the nineteenth century and prohibited any avant-garde experiments'. This was particularly disastrous for poetry, since poets had been experimenting for several decades. Now they were 'paralysed' [168 *pp. 456–7*]. After 1948 all cultural producers were forced into state-run associations, outside which there was no possibility of making a living. Independent literary journals were closed down, to be replaced by publications exclusively propagating the doctrines of socialist realism.

There are also several overarching psychological aspects of East European Stalinism which do not fall precisely within the above categories. First, there is the adulation, and imitation, of all things Soviet, and in particular at this time the Soviet leader, Joseph Stalin. Révai explained what this meant in the cultural field in 1951: 'Soviet culture is the model, the schoolmaster of our new socialist culture. We can absorb and use the rich experience of the Soviet Communist Party not only in the economy and the techniques of class struggle, but also in the creation of a new socialist culture' [55 *p. 194*]. There are many details which reveal the imitative character of East European Stalinism. The Soviet city of Magnitogorsk was regarded as the model of a new industrial centre; it was deliberately built without churches. The Polish city of Nowa Huta, another new industrial centre, was also built without churches. Montias comments, in his comparison of the Soviet and Polish economies: 'I cannot think of any essential difference between Polish and Soviet economic institutions between 1950 and 1955 outside the farm sector' [169 *p. ix*].

Adulation of the Soviet Union naturally went together with the cult of Stalin. This reached absurd heights when the dictator's seventieth birthday approached in 1949. In Hungary a competition was held for the best design of a statue of the Soviet dictator. This was a dangerous honour. An unsuccessful attempt to portray him might well cause offence and lead to the sculptor's imprisonment. The victor, Sándor Mikus, paid for his victory with bad dreams: 'Often at night Stalin's face appears to me. I turn on the light and draw the traits of his face' [55 *p. 198*]. Imitation of the Soviet model was enforced throughout Eastern Europe by a campaign against national communism, which began after Yugoslavia's defiance became known. The anti-Tito resolution passed on 28 June 1948 at the second meeting of the

Cominform was intended to rule out any idea of a specific national road to socialism [17 *pp. 611–21*].

The second characteristic psychological feature is the atmosphere of suspicion and paranoia towards the West and towards enemies and alleged spies in general. This meant in turn an expanded role for the organs of state security, sometimes referred to as the secret police, whose activities of surveillance, repression of non-communists and later purges of communists, were at their height at this time. The purges are so important that they deserve to be examined in a separate section.

These are the main general features of Stalinism in Eastern Europe. There were also some variations in their application. Centralization, for instance, was not applied universally. It occurred in Czechoslovakia (where Slovak autonomy was destroyed), but not in Romania (where an attempt was made to conciliate the large Hungarian minority and an Autonomous Hungarian Region was eventually set up). The cult of the leader, in imitation of the cult of Stalin in the Soviet Union, could be seen in Hungary (Rákosi), Czechoslovakia (Gottwald), Romania (Gheorghiu-Dej) and Bulgaria (where Chervenkov 'bathed in the reflected light of Stalin's personality cult' [104 *p. 108*]) but not in Poland, where Bierut was a relatively shadowy figure.

Finally, it should be pointed out that the communists of Eastern Europe thought of themselves as engaging in a process of modernization. They aimed to rationalize industrial production, bring order to the provision of services to the people, increase educational opportunity, create a more urban environment, expand the sciences, and bring culture to the majority of the people through more effective use of the media. The ruthless measures taken during the Stalin period were intended to create a modern, efficient and prosperous society. Whether and to what extent they succeeded in these aims is a question we shall discuss in Chapter 7 of this book.

## THE PURGES

There were many purges during the early period of communist rule, and they took place for a whole range of reasons. First, the ruling group purged political opponents, then they attacked 'socially undesirable people' such as members of the former middle classes or prosperous farmers who opposed collectivization. Finally, after 1948, the purges extended to communists who had either fallen foul of the existing leaders, or were simply scapegoats chosen to satisfy Stalin that vigilance was being exercised.

Let us start with the immediate postwar purges. Bulgaria was the scene of the most ruthless purge of all. Between December 1944 and March 1945 'People's Courts', set up by the Fatherland Front government, condemned to death three ex-Regents of the country, two ex-Premiers, one ex-Minister of the Interior, 25 ex-cabinet ministers, 68 parliamentary deputies, and a further 2,000 smaller fry [*59 pp. 292–3*]. These publicly announced executions were accompanied by other silent acts of repression. The total number of victims has been estimated by Phyllis Auty at between 20,000 and 100,000 [*26 p. 30*]. The Bulgarian purge cannot be explained as a punishment for collaborators or war criminals. Bulgaria was an ally of Germany during the Second World War but it did not fall under direct German control; the Bulgarian army did not fight on Germany's side; and the repressions carried out by the royal government until 1943 and the subsequent regency were far less brutal than in other countries. The subject has not so far received the investigation it deserves. Were the purges a belated act of communist revenge for the White Terror of 1923 [*106 p. 10*]? Were they a way of liquidating potential political opponents, thus making up for the Nazis' failure to destroy the Bulgarian intelligentsia during the war [*107 p. 186*]? Were they a spontaneous outburst of popular anger? Were the purges encouraged by the Soviet authorities? Any explanation can only be speculative. In any case, this was a purge of the former political right and centre. It did not affect the non-communist left; their turn was to come later.

The Bulgarian purge was an extreme case, but it was not the only one. In Yugoslavia, 100,000 collaborators were killed in 1945–46 [*188 pp. 223–4*]. In Czechoslovakia, 'People's Courts' condemned 20,000 people to prison and executed 400, in 1945 and 1946. In Hungary, 'People's Tribunals' condemned 11,600 to prison and executed 430 between 1945 and 1948. Usually the purges were managed by local political police forces set up by the communists after 1945 for this purpose. In Hungary, the ÁVO (State Defence Department), set up in December 1944, was 'a bizarre mixture of former Arrow Cross thugs and survivors from the concentration camps'. Both groups were ready to act brutally, the former through natural inclination, the latter out of bitterness and desire to take revenge on Hungarians who had supported Nazism [*150 p. 171*]. Every country had its dreaded set of initials, modelled on the Soviet MGB* (Ministry of State Security). Poland had its UB* (Security Office); Czechoslovakia its StB* (State Security); East Germany had its Political Sections, or K–Fives, set up in 1945 as a nucleus for the later *Staatssicherheitsdienst** (known more commonly as the *Stasi*). Yugoslavia had the OZNA (Bureau for the People's Protection). In Romania there was a Special Information Service, later (August 1948) converted into the DGSP* (General Directorate of Popular Security), which subsequently achieved notoriety as the *Securitate* [*174 p. 351*].

The purges of the Stalin era were largely police actions ordered from the top. There were few exceptions to this rule. They could be seen in Czechoslovakia, where the Action Committees set up as a backdrop to the coup of February 1948 played some part between then and May in removing members of the 'bourgeois', non-communist parties from public life, and Bulgaria, where the bloodletting of 1944–45 is described by Nissan Oren as an arbitrary settlement of accounts marked by 'anarchic outbursts of killing' [113 *p. 88*].

The post-1948 purges were often directed against former Social Democrats who had joined the communist party. The key date here was May 1949 when László Rajk, leading Hungarian communist and Foreign Minister, was arrested. The Hungarian leader, Rákosi, was the driving force behind this. The Soviet specialist sent in to investigate, MGB General Fyodor Belkin, reported that Rajk had not committed any serious crime; Rákosi appealed over his head to Stalin, who instructed Belkin to cooperate. Even then, Stalin refused to advise Rajk's execution; here too Rákosi was directly responsible [154 *p. 7, n. 7*]. The Rajk trial led to the purging of 350,000 people, the imprisonment of 150,000, and the execution of 2,000. The purgers started at the top with the former Social Democratic leaders. No distinction was made between right-wingers and left-wingers. György Marosán, who had used his position in 1948 to push Hungarian Social Democracy into merging with communism, was rewarded by Rákosi with five years in prison. One might describe this as political ingratitude of a high order.

Another purge, roughly simultaneous, was against the communist leaders themselves. Some were suspected of sympathy for Tito's Yugoslavia, or more generally of wanting to pursue a distinctive national road to communism. As we have seen, this was perfectly acceptable between 1945 and 1947. Now it was dangerous even to mention such an idea. In Poland, Władysław Gomułka was removed from office and forced to recant errors of this kind in September 1948. He was replaced as party leader by Bolesław Bierut. Gomułka was sent to prison but escaped with his life, partly because of his forthright self-defence and refusal to admit any of the more serious accusations brought against him, but partly also because, in purging Gomułka, Bierut was not acting on Stalin's orders but engaging in a bit of private enterprise. Hence there was no pressure from the Kremlin for a more severe punishment [*Doc. 15*] [58 *p. 152*; 164 *pp. 438–50*]. In Hungary, the campaign against nationalism and Titoism led to the purging of veteran communists such as Kádár, Losonczy and Donáth, who were not of course guilty of anything but were not trusted by Rákosi. János Kádár, the most prominent victim, resisted torture but confessed to imaginary crimes when he was told that this would be for the good of the communist party. He was given four years' imprisonment. In Bulgaria in 1949, Traicho Kostov was successively removed from the leadership, arrested, tortured, given a show trial and hanged. The script for the trial was supplied by Moscow. Unusually, Kostov did not keep to it, retracting his confession in open court. Even that degree of courage, however, did not resist further torture after an adjournment of the proceedings.

A third and final wave of purges took place in 1952–53. This occurred in the context of the anti-Zionist campaign mounted by Stalin in the Soviet

Union; it was noticeable that the victims were usually Jewish. A subsidiary theme in this final purge was the decline in Beria's ministerial position with overall responsibility for the Soviet police and intelligence apparatus. By this time Stalin had lost confidence in Beria; so his rivals, particularly General A.A. Epishev, who had been promoted to Moscow as one of Khrushchev's men from Ukraine, had a chance to destroy him [42 *p. 158*]. Both in Czechoslovakia and Romania the party leaders purged in 1952 were Beria's appointees. In Czechoslovakia, the trial of Rudolf Slánský, General Secretary of the party, was mounted in November, with the active help of Aleksei Beschastnov, an MGB officer who was another of Khrushchev's protégés [42 *p. 169*]; in Romania, Ana Pauker and Vasile Luca, the Romanian Minister of Finance, were dismissed in July. Pauker was spared, but Luca was put on trial and condemned to death in 1954 [176 *pp. 141–2*].

It is hard to find a good explanation for the post-1948 purges of communists, except in the case of Albania where the trial and execution of Koçi Xoxe for Titoism in 1949 was Enver Hoxha's way of proclaiming that he had freed himself from Yugoslavia and would henceforth be leaning towards the Soviet Union. One possible explanation is that the purges were used to settle outstanding scores with former deviationists who had been readmitted to communist parties in the relatively relaxed atmosphere of 1945. This was certainly the case with Vlado Clementis, expelled from the CPCz in 1941 for Slovak nationalism, then readmitted, then finally sacked from the post of Foreign Minister in March 1950, arrested in February 1951, and tried and hanged alongside Slánský in 1952. In Bulgaria, too, Kostov's trial and execution (December 1949) was followed by the expulsion of former leftists who had defied Georgi Dimitrov after 1934 [112 *p. 72*]. Another reason for the purges, from Stalin's point of view, was that the West was stepping up its pressure on communist Eastern Europe in 1949. A policy report of 8 December 1949 from the US National Security Council advised: 'The time is ripe to place greater emphasis on the offensive ... to eliminate or at least reduce predominant Soviet influence in the satellites' [9 *p. 43*]. There was even some evidence that the West might be moving from words to deeds (it had no intention of doing this, but the perception was important). The Albanians alleged that they had foiled an attempt to invade their country in October 1949 and, according to Berman, speaking in November, the Polish authorities caught some Western agents who had infiltrated his country [17 *p. 741*]. A purge of communists whose loyalty was doubtful was a useful preventive measure. This was, it must be admitted, a gigantic overreaction on Stalin's part to a minuscule threat.

Apart from their role in intra-party conflicts and as instruments to secure obedience through terror, the purges also had a certain rationality in economic terms. They provided a useful forced labour supplement to the country's normal labour force, at a time of rapid economic development and labour shortage. Labour camps were set up everywhere. In 1952, Hungary had 120,000 forced labourers in camps and Bulgaria had 100,000. For Romania, only the number of camps is known (97) [*65 pp. 35, 120, 134*]. Poland had 50,000 camp inmates in 1954 [*160 p. 479*]. In Czechoslovakia, the authorities initially hoped there would be 150,000 inmates, but the 'popular movement against reactionaries' failed to develop: the local authorities dragged their feet, and it was left to the courts. It turned out that the Czechoslovak labour camps only held 22,000 [*124 p. 136*]. This is a subject historians of Eastern Europe have only recently started to examine more closely.

## PRESSURE FROM OUTSIDE: COMINFORM AND COMECON

Two kinds of international pressure were exerted on the Eastern European People's Democracies after 1948: political and economic. Politically the Cominform (or Information Bureau) was an instrument of pressure on the ruling parties through its periodic meetings. But it was not intended to be a newer version of the Communist International. Relations between Moscow and the communist parties continued to be regulated bilaterally, as they had been since 1943. The purpose of the Cominform was initially (at its first conference in September 1947) to lay the groundwork for an accelerated seizure of power by the East European communist parties, and later (at its second and third conferences in 1948 and 1949) to condemn Yugoslavia and fire the starting-pistol for a worldwide campaign against Tito and the notion of 'separate national roads to communism'. After 1949 the Cominform's life 'as a political organ came to an end for all practical purposes', although it was not actually wound up until 1956 [*17 p. xx*].

The economic counterpart of the Cominform was Comecon\*, or to give it its full title the CMEA\* (Council for Mutual Economic Assistance), which held its first session in Moscow in April 1949. There has been some controversy over the role and effectiveness of the CMEA in its initial stages. Van Brabant considered that the CMEA's activities 'came to a complete standstill' between 1950 and 1954 [*97 p. 47*], whereas Kaser refers to a secret November 1950 session, held at Hollóháza in Hungary, at which the Soviet representative demanded an upward revision of 'plan targets for heavy industry to meet the requirements of the Korean War' [*78 pp. 49–50*]. Karel Kaplan, working from the original documents, essentially took Kaser's view. He noted that the November 1950 session was 'the last meeting of the Council for four years' [*77 p. 24*], but added that the important decisions were made in the narrower Bureau, which continued to meet, and which was attended by Stalin's close associate Anastas Mikoyan, alongside numerous Soviet economic experts.

The pressure from Comecon had a big impact on economic policy, particularly in Czechoslovakia. Ambitious targets for iron ore extraction and processing, collectivization of agriculture, and above all armaments production were set by it. In fact Kaplan claims that the economies of Eastern Europe were 'directed from a single centre – Moscow' [77 *p. 35*]. Several meetings of the Council and the Bureau were devoted to criticizing Czechoslovakia's failure sufficiently to re-orient its foreign trade away from the West. In September 1949 Eugen Loebl, the Czechoslovak Minister of Foreign Trade, was arrested, partly for this reason. The Czechoslovaks were pressed to provide the necessary industrial equipment and raw materials to other, less developed, Comecon countries [77 *p. 20*]. They were forced to engage in a 'self-criticism' in the CMEA Bureau, and make a dramatic change in their trading patterns. In 1948 only 33 per cent of Czechoslovakia's trade was with CMEA countries, in 1950 the proportion was 54 per cent, and by 1953 it had reached a maximum of 72 per cent [125 *pp. 78–9*].

Another source of disagreement with the Czechoslovaks was the balance between manufacturing and raw material extraction. Stalin wanted to raise targets for the latter; the Czechoslovak delegation claimed that this was impossible as the country was poor in raw materials. But they were forced to give way. In the context of the Korean War the production of armaments was given top priority. In December 1950 Moscow told its East European allies to be prepared for a possible United States invasion of their territory in 1952 [121 *p. 118*]. A month later the First Secretaries and Ministers of Defence of Eastern Europe were given this warning by Stalin: 'The Soviet camp enjoys temporary superiority, for three or four years. ... It will be necessary to make good use of this short period to complete the systematic preparation of our armies by devoting to them all the economic, political and human means at our disposal' [55 *p. 127*]. The next day the Czechoslovaks agreed to adjust their Five Year Plan accordingly [77 *p. 30*].

The less developed countries of Eastern Europe (Bulgaria, Romania and Albania) had less reason to object to Comecon's activities, as they were not disadvantaged by them. For instance, the second meeting of the Comecon Council, held at Sofia in August 1949, resolved to expand multilateral trade among member countries at the expense of trade with the capitalist world. This meant that the economically advanced countries of East Central Europe had to re-direct their trade southwards. The results were dramatic: between 1948 and 1952 the proportion of trade with fellow-members of the CMEA increased from 41 per cent to 67 per cent in Poland, 34 per cent to 71 per cent in Hungary, 71 per cent to 85 per cent in Romania, and 78 per cent to 89 per cent in Bulgaria [86 *p. 41*].

Although it is clear enough that the Comecon Bureau intervened repeatedly in the economic affairs of the member countries, this does not mean that there was any real attempt to establish a rational international division of labour. The fundamental principle was that of autarchic economic development. Stalin himself rejected the idea of plan coordination in

March 1949 [86 *p. 12*]. Not until 1955 was there any move to synchronize the East Europeans' Five Year Plans with those of the USSR. To quote Peter Wiles's witty summary: 'Under Stalin the USSR had the power but not the will to impose economic unity; while under Khrushchev it had the will but not the power' [99 *p. 311*].

# CHAPTER FIVE

# DE-STALINIZATION AND THE CRITICAL YEAR OF 1956

The impact of Stalin's death was felt everywhere in Eastern Europe, but nowhere more strongly than in the German Democratic Republic. It was generally felt in Moscow that it had been a mistake to allow Walter Ulbricht and the SED to strike out a course towards 'the building of socialism'. Lavrenty Beria, who was very influential in the early months of 1953, proposed that the whole project be abandoned, and his colleagues and rivals in the leadership, Molotov and Khrushchev, while not going so far, agreed that the process should be 'slowed down' [42 *p. 192*]. The severely critical approach of the new Soviet government found expression in a series of instructions for a radical change of course [*Doc. 16*]. These were accepted by the SED Politbureau at its session of 5 and 6 June 1953. A communiqué was worked out and issued on 9 June announcing a 'New Course' in domestic policy.

Unfortunately, both the Soviet leaders and their East German counterparts had failed to raise at any time the crucial question of the mass discontent provoked by an increase of 10 per cent in the work norms which the SED was about to introduce, in order to raise productivity. Hence while the regime relaxed its policies towards the Churches, the peasantry and the middle classes, the workers felt they had received nothing. The SED defiantly stuck to the new work norms, announcing on 16 June that they were 'absolutely correct' and would be implemented to the letter [141 *p. 226*]. This set off the rising of 17 June 1953, 65 per cent of the participants in which were working class. Although it eventually turned into an attack on the whole communist regime, initially the 17 June uprising was solely a protest against the increased work norms. Soviet tanks were needed to suppress the rising. Once the dust had settled, it became clear that Walter Ulbricht and his party had in fact gained a new lease of life from these events. The Soviet leaders, who had originally had grave doubts about the viability of communism in East Germany, now decided that they would have to adopt Ulbricht's line of a rapid transition to 'socialism'. The 'New Course' was continued, and various financial concessions were made by the Soviet side, including the ending of reparations payments. Ulbricht was able to see off his rivals in the party, and begin eighteen years of uninterrupted personal rule. But the offending work norms were now rescinded. Throughout the 1950s wages rose faster than productivity in East German industry. So the workers had also gained a victory. To keep their goodwill, the SED 'had to give its workers a virtual veto power over wages, prices and work norms' [135 *p. 11*].

## HUNGARY IN 1956: A CRISIS OUT OF CONTROL

The 'New Course' programme put forward by Imre Nagy in Hungary in his report of 27 June 1953 [*Doc. 17*], and adopted in its main essentials in the Central Committee resolution of 28 June 1953, was not a particularly radical document [*Doc. 18*]. It was very similar to the East German proposals which had been adopted by the SED a fortnight earlier. The role played by Moscow in pressing for change was clear in both cases; it could not be otherwise, since any inner-party opposition had been completely cowed in the previous five years. Nagy pledged to abolish the forced labour camps, to tear up the 'kulak lists', to allow the peasants to leave the collective farms if they wanted to, and to replace the previous stress on heavy industry with a concentration on the production of consumer goods and raising the standard of living. The peasants eagerly seized the opportunity Nagy was giving them: the number of private farms in Hungary increased by 200,000 between 1953 and 1954, and the proportion of arable land held by collective farms fell from 26 per cent to 18 per cent. Real wages increased by 15 per cent. But Imre Nagy was not permitted to continue with this policy.

The reason for this was the tremendous dependence of the Hungarian communist regime on the Soviet Union, which meant that Moscow's own policy vacillations between 1953 and 1956 had a more direct impact than anywhere else (except East Germany, which was similarly dependent). Rákosi had been a particular target of Beria's criticisms when a Hungarian party delegation went to Moscow in June 1953; thus Beria's disgrace and eventual execution in December was advantageous to the former Hungarian Stalinist leader. The New Course itself was closely associated with Khrushchev's rival Malenkov, and the decline in Malenkov's influence during the winter of 1954–55 brought an abrupt end to this phase of Soviet policy. In January 1955 the Hungarians were again summoned to Moscow. This time it was the turn of Imre Nagy to be hauled over the coals. He was accused of denigrating the party's leading role and denying the importance of the class struggle. In March 1955 the HWP* abandoned the New Course, and the flexible agrarian policy advocated by Nagy, and returned to the promotion of heavy industry. Nagy himself was dismissed as Prime Minister in

April, and expelled from the HWP in December. But Rákosi's triumph was incomplete: a group of sympathizers formed around Nagy, mainly veteran communists who had suffered in the previous era, and they refused to surrender to the new line.

They had their opportunity in February 1956 when Khrushchev made his secret speech against Stalin at the Twentieth Party Congress of the Soviet communist party. It was clear that the coming of official de-Stalinization had opened up a space for dissident communist intellectuals in Hungary. Now the party press began to agitate openly for reform. The students and leading intellectuals got together in March 1956 in the 'Petöfi Circle', which began to draw in industrial workers as well in the summer of 1956. Yet Rákosi remained in charge, obstinately clinging on to power. His final master-stroke was a plan to arrest 400 of the main trouble-makers, which he was unable to effect because Moscow forbade it.

The Soviet leaders had at first favoured Rákosi, even after Khrushchev's secret speech. They were very concerned about the activities of the Petöfi Circle, and Soviet Ambassador Yuri Andropov was entirely in favour of a hard line. But in July they changed their minds, partly because the Yugoslav leader Tito made an improvement of relations dependent on the removal of this man he hated (Rákosi had led the verbal attacks on Yugoslavia after 1948), partly because Anastas Mikoyan, a top member of the Soviet leadership, went to Budapest on a fact-finding mission and found out that most of the Politbureau of the Hungarian party thought Rákosi was the main obstacle to the restoration of confidence. Mikoyan told Rákosi to resign. But instead of appointing Nagy as party leader the Hungarian leaders fell back on another member of the old Stalinist guard, Ernő Gerő. Gerő was unwilling to accept the job, on the grounds that he was in poor health, and too associated with Rákosi, but his colleagues insisted [151 *p. 47*].

It immediately became clear that the removal of Rákosi had not brought about any change in policy. In fact the first act of the Gerő leadership was to produce a plan whereby 60 per cent of all cultivated land would be brought into the collective or state sector by 1960. Even Soviet Ambassador Andropov thought this was unnecessarily provocative [19 *p. 250*]. There was a continued refusal to return to the New Course, readmit Nagy to the party or rehabilitate the victims of Stalinist injustice. Andropov also continued to uphold this line of action throughout the summer.

But then, early in October, taking advantage of Gerő's absence on leave, and without consulting Andropov, the other Hungarian party leaders began to make concessions to the rising tide of intellectual protest and working-class discontent. On 6 October they allowed László Rajk, the most prominent victim of the purges of the Stalin era, to receive a state funeral. It was attended by hundreds of thousands of people. On 12 October they arrested the man regarded as chiefly responsible for the conduct of the purges, former

Minister of Defence Mihály Farkas; the next day they readmitted Imre Nagy to the party without demanding that he disavow the views for which he had been expelled. Andropov saw these measures as 'a series of unprincipled retreats by the party, seriously undermining the position of the Hungarian leadership' [19 *p. 194*]. In actual fact it was the lateness of the concessions, and their half-hearted character, that had undermined the HWP's position. The infuriated population began to take more radical steps. On 23 October a demonstration was held in Budapest in support of sixteen demands drawn up by the students of the Budapest Technical University the day before [*Doc. 19*]. It was massive, and at first peaceful, but Gerő, who had now returned to Hungary, poured oil on the flames by calling the demonstrators 'a group of Fascists'. In the evening an attempt was made to storm the radio station. Its ÁVH* defenders opened fire. Meanwhile, Gerő could think of no other way of restoring order than to call in Soviet troops. They arrived in the early hours of 24 October. Between 24 and 28 October there were armed clashes throughout the country [36 *pp. 80–1*].

The obvious inability of the Hungarian Workers' Party to master the situation meant that the decision on what to do next was passed to Moscow. The Soviet leaders, who had just reached an agreement with the Poles, which we shall examine later, did not think the question could or should be re-solved by military force alone. They pressed the Hungarian party to make compromises. Accordingly, on 24 October Nagy was appointed Prime Minister. Gerő was forced to resign as head of the HWP the next day. His replacement was János Kádár. On 27 October Nagy formed a 'People's Patriotic Government'. This body was still dominated by the communists, but it did not include the most notorious followers of Rákosi, and it did include two token non-communist leaders, Béla Kovács and Zoltán Tildy. Eventually (28 October) Nagy persuaded the other party leaders to agree to a truce and offer a change of policy along the lines of some of the Sixteen Points of 22 October (such as the dissolution of the secret police; the restoration of the Hungarian national emblem; and the withdrawal of Soviet troops from Budapest). Everything would now depend on whether the insur-gents, and the Soviet side, accepted this compromise [151 *p. 72*].

There was no reason for the insurgents to refuse. Contrary to the fears and hopes expressed at the time, the Hungarian insurgents of 1956 did not want to put the political clock back to 1945 or 1939. On the contrary, even the leaders of the former centre and right parties, such as the Smallholders, accepted that the socialist system would continue to exist, whatever happened politically. The Hungarian revolution also included a 'left' com-ponent, expressed in the emergence of Workers' Councils. But the predomi-nant ideology of the revolution was best summed up by the former Populist writer István Bibó, who called for a 'third road' between communism and capitalism, in which a multi-party system would exist, but only in so far as it did not threaten the achievements of socialism, and Hungary would be a neutral state attached neither to the East nor the West [*150 pp. 311–12*].

It seemed for a short period of time as if the 'third road' of the Hungarian revolution would be acceptable to the Soviet Union. When Imre Nagy announced the end of the one-party system and formed a cabinet which included leaders of the former Smallholders' Party (30 October) he was under the impression that he had Soviet agreement. We now know that this was so, but only for a short time. A meeting of the Soviet Presidium on 30 October agreed with Khrushchev's suggestion to withdraw troops from Hungary and leave the decisions there to Nagy. The main reasons for this were that such a step appeared to fit in with the policy adopted already towards Poland, where Gomułka had been allowed to take over the party despite the Kremlin's initial opposition; and it also had the full approval of the Chinese Communist Party [*Doc. 22*]. However, they changed their minds the next day.

Even the recent discovery of the minutes of the Presidium's meetings has not completely clarified the reasons for this. If we are to take the arguments presented on 31 October at face value, a strange picture emerges: the main factor was the Suez crisis: the news that Britain and France were about to attack Egypt, a country the Soviet Union regarded as an ally. The Soviet leaders thought they would lose Egypt to the West, that their position in the Middle East would receive a shattering blow, and that to abandon Hungary as well would be too much of a retreat in the face of the imperialists: they would 'understand this as weakness on our part and attack', said Khrushchev. The other reason was pressure from the Chinese leaders, many of whom were present in Moscow throughout this period. They decided overnight that Nagy was making too many concessions to the non-communists and there was a danger of a capitalist restoration.

Finally a letter came from the Italian communist leader Togliatti warning that the Hungarian communists were losing control of the situation [*19 pp. 334–5*]. Alarming reports of the lynching of ÁVH personnel strengthened this feeling. These disturbing developments strengthened the hand of hard-liners such as Molotov. The Soviet troop withdrawals, begun on 30 October, were stopped a day later, and fresh troops were brought in. Imre Nagy now faced a choice. Either he could take charge of the restoration of party authority and destroy the revolution, or he could abandon the party and try to save the revolution. He took the latter course, declaring Hungary's neutrality and withdrawal from the Warsaw Pact on 1 November.

This step set the stage for the final act of the Hungarian tragedy. Given the West's practical acceptance that Hungary was in the Soviet sphere, and the great imbalance of military strength between Hungary and the Soviet Union, the success of Soviet military intervention was a foregone conclusion. The majority of the Hungarian army avoided taking part in any battles, to avoid spilling blood pointlessly. The fight was continued by the insurgent groups which had sprung up during the first Soviet intervention. Soviet troops went into action against Budapest on 4 November. By the end of the day most of the city had been seized. Three main centres of resistance remained, with roughly 1,000 insurgents in each of them. By 12 November it was all over. Hungary was reconquered, in the name of the new communist government set up by János Kádár.

Kádár returned to Budapest in a Soviet armoured car on 7 November 1956. Kovrig comments: 'Seldom has a government assumed office in less propitious circumstances' [150 p. 317]. The Kádár government was dependent almost entirely on the Soviet occupying authorities, and had to fight on two fronts, against pressure from the returned Stalinists, who wanted to go back on all the post-1953 reforms, and against initially unanimous opposition from the Hungarian people themselves. To most people's surprise, Kádár was able to tread this tightrope successfully. On the one hand, there was repression: roughly 2,000 people were executed, including Nagy himself, and many others were sentenced to long prison terms. On the other hand, Kádár legalized the Workers' Councils that had emerged during the revolution, and he negotiated with them seriously for some months. (Eventually, in November 1957, he felt strong enough to abolish them.) The most discredited Stalinists were firmly kept out of the Politbureau, and the June 1957 party conference of the re-founded and renamed HSWP* resolved to call on non-party people wherever possible to help in the work of reconstruction. In 1963 a general amnesty was issued for most of those sentenced to offences arising out of the events of 1956 [151 p. 188].

## POLAND IN 1956: A CRISIS MASTERED

The reaction in Poland to the process of de-Stalinization in the USSR was essentially the same as in Hungary, but the outcome was very different. This was a result of the weakness of the Stalinist faction. Whereas in Hungary Imre Nagy was isolated in the communist leadership, and excessively dependent on Moscow's decision to force his appointment as Prime Minister, in Poland the Stalinists and their opponents were evenly divided. Hence the fall of Malenkov and the apparent end of the New Course had little effect, beyond preserving a stalemate. The really decisive event in Poland was the Twentieth Party Congress of the CPSU*. Khrushchev's secret speech at the Congress quickly became common knowledge, as it was printed and distributed in 20,000 copies by the Warsaw City Party Committee, as well as being sent over the airwaves by the *Voice of America* for those who dared to listen.

The two main factions in the ruling party, the PZPR*, began to take organized shape at this point. The Stalinists are normally referred to as the Natolinians, the reformers as the Puławians. The First Secretary of the party,

Eduard Ochab, who replaced Bierut after the latter's death in March 1956, endeavoured to hold the balance, inclining now one way, and now the other. The pressure from below was strong, and unlike in Hungary a considerable section of the party leadership was responsive to this. Hence the contrasting behaviour of the Soviet leaders. In Hungary they intervened in mid-1956 to push the reform process forwards. In Poland they intervened to hold it back.

The situation in Poland reached a critical stage with the Poznań riots of June 1956, which arose from the failure of the government to satisfy the demands of the workers of the Stalin Works, which was the largest industrial enterprise in the country. The demonstrations in Poznań were so large and violent that they could only be put down with the use of troop reinforcements from Warsaw. The official figures for people killed and wounded were 53 and 300 respectively [167 *p. 350*]. The Poznań workers had been crushed, but a movement for reform began within the PZPR itself. This grew stronger through the summer of 1956. The situation was serious enough to compel Bulganin to visit Warsaw. Once there he threw his weight on the side of the Natolin, or conservative, faction of the party.

In October 1956, when the pressure from below became overwhelming, with the formation of Workers' Councils, the Soviet leaders again tried to intervene to hold back the movement. But when it became clear that the conservative faction was rapidly losing influence in the PZPR, and that the call for the return of Gomułka to power was irresistible, the Soviet leaders were wise enough to concede the point. In any case, the concessions made in October 1956 were less far-reaching than they appeared. The new head of the party – Gomułka – was known as a convinced and dedicated communist, who would not give way on the essentials of party control and the alliance between Poland and the Soviet Union. Everything else was in fact negotiable. Gomułka insisted on three conditions before he agreed to take over the leadership of the party: the decollectivization of agriculture, the ending of Soviet control over the Polish army and a defusing of the conflict with the Catholic Church. The Soviet leaders gave way on all three points. The peasants started to leave the collective farms, Marshal Rokossowski was sent home to Moscow and all Soviet advisers to the army were recalled. Cardinal Wyszyński, the Roman Catholic Primate, was freed on 28 October [173].

A further feature of the Polish October, not mentioned in the discussions with the Soviet leaders, was the spontaneous development of Workers' Councils. Gomułka himself held no brief for such institutions, in fact he saw them as a dangerous anarchist diversion. He was unable to suppress them at first, so he had to give some concessions. The November 1956 law on Workers' Councils stated that

> Workers' Councils, elected by all employees, will fulfil the function of the general management of enterprises. The director of an enterprise will be

appointed by the authorities in agreement with the Workers' Council and will be responsible jointly to the authorities and the Workers' Council. The director cannot be appointed without the consent of the Workers' Council. Wages will be settled jointly by the Workers' Council and the trade union committee. [70 *pp. 42–3*]

Over the next few years, however, the position of these Councils was gradually undermined. Finally, in 1958, they were deprived of all independence by being merged with Conferences of Workers' Self-Management (KSRs*), on which party nominees had a permanent majority through the inclusion of representatives of the trade unions, the youth organization and the party itself [81 *p. 101*].

Khrushchev conceded most of the Poles' demands in 1956. In the last resort he was confident that the new Polish leaders would be able to keep the situation under control, and that they were not anti-Soviet [11 *p. 205*]. This was certainly true of Gomułka. He regarded the concessions of 1956 as a partial and temporary retreat, not a definitive move away from communism. In subsequent years he rescinded most of them, and by the mid-1960s little was left of the extensive political reforms of 1956.

Gomułka tended to rely after 1956 on members of the conservative Natolin faction of the party, such as Zenon Nowak, rather than the liberals who had brought him to power. Later on he aligned himself with the rising nationalist wing under Mieczysław Moczar, who was appointed head of state security in 1959 and Minister of the Interior in 1964. In the cultural sphere the revisionist intellectuals came under attack almost immediately. In October 1957 Gomułka proclaimed that 'the revisionist wing must be cut off from the party' [36 *p. 102*]. By the end of 1958, 28,000 members had been expelled; in 1959, Professor Kołakowski, the leading revisionist philosopher, was dismissed from his position as editor of the main Polish journal of philosophy and in 1966 he was expelled from the PZPR. The revisionist journals *Przegląd Kulturalny* and *Nowa Kultura* were subjected to censorship from 1957. In 1963 they were forced to cease publication entirely, being replaced by a new, harmless journal which would not 'cause ideological confusion'. This is not to say that Poland ceased to be unusual. Gomułka himself summed up Poland's individuality very well in 1963: the independence of the peasantry and the strength of the Catholic Church meant that the country was further away from socialism than other parts of Eastern Europe [*Doc. 23*]. One distinctive trait he did not mention in his speech was the determination and bravery of the cultural dissidents, who protested in 1964 (the Letter of the Thirty-Four against press censorship), in 1965 (Kuroń and Modzelewski's *Open Letter to the Party*, which brought them prison sentences of three and three-and-a-half years respectively), and in 1966 (the protest of the Twenty-Two against the expulsion of Kołakowski).

# CHAPTER SIX

# A DECADE OF CONSOLIDATION

### DIVERGENT DEVELOPMENTS

The period after 1956 was characterized by two contrasting features: a growing diversity within the region, and an increasing tendency towards the consolidation of the post-Stalinist system in its partially reformed shape. We shall look first at diversity, which was partly a result of the re-emergence of cultural and economic differences overlaid in the 1950s by the Stalinist carapace of uniformity, though it also resulted from differing rates of reform and liberalization in the post-Stalin epoch. One startling divergence that developed in the northern part of the region after 1956 was the contrast between the political and cultural ferment in Hungary and Poland, and the quiescence of the Czechoslovaks and East Germans.

Poland and Hungary belong together in many ways. As we saw in Chapter 5, they both experienced upheavals in 1956; and although their respective crises developed very differently over the course of the year, the end result was essentially the same. In Hungary, a period of severe repression was followed fairly rapidly by moves towards liberalization in all areas. In December 1961, János Kádár neatly reversed the Rákosi regime's slogan, which was 'Those who are not with us are against us'. Instead of this, he put forward his own version: 'Those who are not against us are with us' [148 p. 264]. Gradually and cautiously, in the course of the 1960s, the HSWP moved to expand the area of toleration. In 1966 it sanctioned the publication of works 'that are more or less in opposition to Marxism or socialist realism as long as they possess humanistic value', and it divided cultural production into the three categories of supported, tolerated and prohibited. The Budapest School of Marxists, people like András Hegedűs, Ferenc Fehér and Ágnes Heller, who were all followers of George Lukács, the veteran communist philosopher who had supported the 1956 revolution, began to investigate Hungarian society in a critical way, using the insights of modern sociology. The phase of relative intellectual freedom lasted until 1974, when many reformers in high places were dismissed and those they had protected were forced into silence or exile.

In Poland, the period of free activity and substantial concessions, which was the main achievement of the agitation of 1956, came to an end much earlier, thanks to a creeping restoration of controls over most areas of public life. Gomułka regarded the domestic concessions of 1956 as a temporary retreat: he was no liberal, and he intended to resume his 'advance towards socialism' as soon as practically possible. But he was realistic. Decollectivization was not reversed. Instead, the government attempted to discourage the peasants who had left the collectives in 1956 by channelling agricultural investment towards the state farms. Similarly, the improved post-1956 position of the Roman Catholic Church was not seriously undermined, but the state cut down on the building of new churches. Between 1956 and 1969 only 27 new churches were built, at a time when there was both considerable population growth and substantial migration from country to town. The government also taxed Church property and refused to hand over ecclesiastical possessions it had confiscated from the Germans in 1945. None of this amounted to a serious anti-religious campaign. In general, Poland was the only East European country where the 1960s saw an actual diminution of political and cultural freedom; but to keep this in perspective one should remember that, even so, by 1965 it was still 'much ahead of most, if not all, of the members of the Soviet bloc in political liberalism' (Brus) [81 p. 76]. Admittedly, things got worse after 1967, with the campaign against Zionism and the resultant emigration of two-thirds of the surviving Jewish population.

In foreign policy, Gomułka saw Poland as circumscribed by its geographical position. As he remarked in December 1956: 'People who criticise us ... would perhaps suggest that we shift the geopolitical situation of Poland, moving it to another part of the globe, or even another planet' [36 p. 101]. What this implied was a continued close alliance with the Soviet Union and support for Soviet initiatives.

No one has really given a convincing explanation for the immunity of Czechoslovakia from the changes that swept over the communist world between the death of Stalin in 1953 and the fall of Khrushchev in 1964. Many writers take the view that material issues were decisive. Here, for example, is Sharon Wolchik: 'The Czechoslovak economy continued to perform well in the 1950s, because it was not as severely affected as Poland and Hungary by the Stalinist model of development. This is why economic discontent was not as pervasive' [39 p. 133].

There are, however, some problems with this interpretation. The Czechoslovak economy was not crisis-free. There was a severe setback to economic growth in the early 1960s. This crisis is usually seen as the result of distortions in the system, in particular an unbalanced pattern of investment, resulting from the Stalinist economic model itself. Moreover, even before this, the working population had grounds for discontent. At 1.7 per cent per annum between 1951 and 1956 and 4.6 per cent per annum between 1956 and 1960 the rate of growth of real wages in Czechoslovakia was lower in the 1950s than in any other East European country [81 *pp. 64, 95*].

Another explanation sometimes put forward for the absence of change in Czechoslovakia is the allegedly widespread support of the people for communism, as evidenced by the results of the free elections held in 1946. But the terrible Stalinist years had largely obliterated the socialist aspirations of the 1940s. The intellectuals, for their part, who played a key role in Hungary and Poland, generally kept out of the limelight in Czechoslovakia, after a brief flurry of activity in 1956. They were rebuked by Novotný in June 1957 for indulging in 'imperialist propaganda', and after that they fell silent [36 *p. 119*]. It is hard to say why. Perhaps there was some residual support left over from the pre-1948 era, when Czechoslovak intellectuals in their thousands had flocked to join the CPCz.

Two further reasons for the absence of reform seem more persuasive than the ones considered above: fear, and the lack of an alternative power centre. First, fear. As we have seen, the final wave of purges in Czechoslovakia was more extensive and ruthless than elsewhere, and it lasted longer, well into 1954. The second reason was also connected with the purges. Anyone from the earlier communist generation who was not an utter mediocrity was removed from the scene in the early 1950s. Antonín Novotný, who was mediocrity personified, took over from the Stalinist leader Gottwald on his death in 1953. Only the colourless figure of Antonín Zapotocký was in a position to challenge him, and Zapotocký's own early death quickly ended this episode. Genuine reform had to await the coming of a new generation, brought up in the communist environment, who reformed not through hatred of the system but through confidence that it could be improved – the generation of Alexander Dubček. We shall examine the fate of Dubček's reforms in more detail below.

The fourth member of the northern group of communist countries was the German Democratic Republic. Its uniqueness lay in its geographical position, on the front line of the conflict between East and West, and its artificiality as a state. As we saw in Chapter 5, in the early 1950s the grudging approval of Stalin was won for the 'construction of socialism' on the eastern part of the territory of Germany. This amounted to abandoning the goal of re-unification. The mini-state thus created was run by the SED and its leader, Walter Ulbricht, as a very tight ship. Order was Ulbricht's highest value; the intellectuals who took advantage of the space provided by Khrushchev's de-Stalinization moves of 1956 were brought back into line in 1957 with a campaign against 'revisionism'. The opposition within the party leadership to Ulbricht's hard line was dealt with in 1958: a number of high-ranking party officials, including Politbureau members Karl Schirdewan and Fred Oelssner and Minister of State Security Erich Wollweber, were publicly criticized and demoted to minor administrative positions. After this there was no further opposition, either from above or below.

This stability was promoted in the short term by the GDR's exposed international position. A major series of East–West crises over the status of Berlin took place between 1958 and 1961. They were brought to an end in August 1961 with the only solution that would guarantee both a defusing of international tension and the continuing existence of the GDR as a communist state: the building of a wall to bring to an end the flow of emigrants to the West. Until August 1961 the citizens of the GDR were able to move easily to West Germany if they were dissatisfied with their lives; after the Berlin Wall had been built they were prohibited from doing so, and if they tried to flee they had to run the gauntlet of border guards who would shoot on sight; if they were not shot they were punished for the crime of 'fleeing from the republic'.

Behind the Berlin Wall and the fortified border that ran the length of the country, Ulbricht and the SED were able to continue the 'construction of socialism', safe in the knowledge that they now had an absolute guarantee of Soviet support in doing so. It was not sufficient to block the exit route to the West, however. Mental attitudes had to be changed. As Kurt Hager wrote in May 1963: 'We have blocked the militarists with the wall, but they must also be blocked on the mental level. There must be an anti-Fascist barrier in everyone's head' [140a *p. 141*]. This implied strict controls over the media, and a serious effort to stop West German broadcasts from reaching East German television sets. The youth movement was set to work to re-align the television aerials in what was called a 'Lightning Action against NATO Transmitters'. But this was not enough. The rulers of the GDR were well aware that to secure any kind of acquiescence from the population they would have to provide access to the consumer goods increasingly taken for granted in the West. In this they were actually remarkably successful, as the following figures demonstrate: between 1960 and 1970 the proportion of East Germans with television sets rose from 17 per cent to 69 per cent. The corresponding figures for refrigerators are 6 per cent to 56 per cent, and for washing machines 6 per cent to 54 per cent. By 1970 even motor cars were within reach: 16 out of 100 families possessed one, although the average waiting time was seven years. This material progress, combined with effective and all-embracing surveillance by the state security organization, the *Stasi*, produced at least the appearance of a stable and well-founded regime.

Looking further south, striking contrasts developed after 1956 between all the Balkan countries. Bulgaria differed simply because unlike the others it strove under its ruler Todor Zhivkov to follow the example of the Soviet Union in all respects [32 *p. 315*]. Zhivkov repeatedly proclaimed his country's complete alignment with Moscow in the most extravagant terms.

As he declared in May 1962: 'Our political watch-dial is exact to the second with the watch of the Soviet Union. Our watch is working towards Moscow time. This is a matter of great pride for all Bulgarian people' [106 *p. 129*]. He was still singing the same tune a decade later: 'Bulgaria and the Soviet Union' he said in September 1973, 'will act as a single body, breathing with the same lungs and nourished with the same bloodstream' [107 *p. 199*].

His subservience helped him to achieve sole power in the early 1960s and then allowed him to survive the replacement of Khrushchev as Soviet leader by Brezhnev in 1964. In 1961 his predecessor Chervenkov, who was clearly identified with the Stalin period, was removed, in the context of the second wave of de-Stalinization initiated by Khrushchev at the Twenty-Second Party Congress of the CPSU; a year later Zhivkov was able to see off his chief rival for the succession, Anton Yugov. In May 1962 Khrushchev visited Sofia and made it clear that he preferred Zhivkov. Later on, in November, Zhivkov went directly to Moscow, returning with permission to remove Yugov from the Politbureau. After this there were no more threats to Zhivkov's supremacy in Bulgaria.

Albania's foreign policy course was exactly the reverse of Bulgaria's, though its internal political and economic system was not very different. Albania took the Chinese side in the Sino-Soviet dispute which blew up in 1960. One reason for this was the fear that the Soviet reconciliation with Tito would lead Khrushchev to abandon Stalin's policy of supporting Albania against Yugoslav claims. Khrushchev reacted to this disobedience by breaking off relations with Albania. In a speech in October 1961 he went so far as to refer to the 'bloody misdeeds of Enver Hoxha' and he prophesied that the time would come 'when the Albanian people will have their say, and then the Albanian leaders will have to answer for the harm they have done their country' [189 *p. 132*]. The Albanian communists were able to survive the consequences of this because they had no common frontier with the Soviet Union, firm Chinese support and, in the person of Hoxha, a leader who was an astute political survivor, although their proud isolation did not improve the standard of living in what remained by far the poorest country in Europe.

Romania went over to a form of 'national communism' during the 1960s. Domestically, increased stress was placed on national values in the cultural sphere. This move was already well in train before Nicolae Ceauşescu took over in 1965. His predecessor, Gheorghe Gheorghiu-Dej, had already excluded Russian language teaching from the schools, and rehabilitated Romanian national heroes vilified during the Stalin period. In 1963 anti-Russian remarks made by Karl Marx in some *Notes on the Rumanians,* discovered by a Polish scholar, were published in Romania. The official *History of Romania* was also revised between 1960 and 1964, the result being a work which stressed the unimportance of the Hungarian settlements in Transylvania and the repeated misdeeds of Russian imperialists during the nineteenth century [179 *p. 50*]. The cultural and administrative autonomy enjoyed by the Hungarian minority in Transylvania was whittled down from 1956 onwards. In 1960 the boundaries of the Hungarian autonomous district were redrawn, reducing the Hungarian element to 62 per cent; in 1965 Romania was declared a unitary state; finally, in 1968 a reform of local government resulted in the complete elimination of Hungarian autonomy.

Romania also pursued an independent foreign policy. This had two aspects: economic and political. In the economic sphere Gheorghiu-Dej defied pressure from the Soviet Union to move towards closer integration with the other countries of the CMEA. This was because Khrushchev's proposed international division of labour would have prevented Romania from continuing its programme of Stalinist industrialization. The new arrangements would have placed it permanently in the position of a supplier of raw materials to the more advanced communist economies. A Romanian statement issued in March 1963 rejected these proposals; Khrushchev chose not to press the issue. In July 1963 a Moscow CMEA meeting permitted Romania to continue its industrialization programme without further interference. In the political sphere, the Romanian leader was determined both to stay neutral in the dispute between the Soviet Union and China and to get on better terms with the capitalist West. His successor Ceauşescu continued this approach. In 1967 Romania entered diplomatic relations with West Germany, following this up a few months later by refusing to join the Eastern bloc countries in breaking ties with Israel. None of this made any difference to the fundamental political and social structure of the country, or threatened the exclusive rule of the communist party, which is perhaps why Romania's defiance was not seen as a sufficient reason for Soviet intervention.

The most distinctive policy of all was pursued by Yugoslavia, which was understandable given that country's almost complete freedom from Soviet pressure after 1948. Yet, paradoxically, the first thought of the Yugoslav leaders after the outbreak of the quarrel with Stalin was to continue on a 'Marxist-Leninist' path without and against the leading Marxist-Leninist. This period of obstinate orthodoxy lasted for two years. Then, beginning in 1950, the Yugoslav communists started to develop their own distinctive brand of Marxism. For the historian, the important question at this juncture is the relation of ideology to policy, of theory to practice. In theory, the Yugoslavs were preparing a set of extremely far-reaching changes. The prime mover here was Milovan Djilas. He advocated going over to the management of enterprises through Workers' Councils. Tito responded to the suggestion with enthusiasm, as Djilas later recalled: "'Giving the factories to the workers" he said , "but this is Marxist!" and he agreed to do it' [3 *p. 269*]. The communist party was turned into a 'League of Communists of Yugoslavia' (LCY)* in 1952, as a symbolic expression of fact that it would implement its 'leading role' in society 'not by decree' as in the past but by 'political and ideological education' [185 *p. 177*]. That was the theory. The practice was rather different. The degree of autonomy allowed to each enterprise clearly depended on how centralized the planning system was. Only with the gradual reduction in central state control of the economy after the reform of 1965 did the system of self-management through Workers' Councils become a reality. Moreover, the LCY retained its monopoly of power and of all key governmental positions. Tito remained the untouchable autocrat. There were limits on freedom of the press. Dissidents were punished, though less severely than in other Eastern European countries [36 *pp. 74–5*].

Communist Yugoslavia evolved away from Stalinism in the 1950s and 1960s by a series of advances and retreats. There have been several attempts to explain these shifts of policy. Joseph Rothschild has put forward the idea of a 'dialectic' in which each major tide of reform was accompanied by a 'riptide' from forces opposed to it [54 *p. 183*]; Ross Johnson uses the model of a 'shifting triangle', in which domestic policy was determined by changes in Yugoslav relations with the Soviet Union, with periods of closer relations with the USSR associated with domestic rigidity, and periods of conflict with flexibility and reform [186]. But the interrelation of domestic and foreign policy, if it existed at all, was much more complex than this. It should not be forgotten that Yugoslavia's conflict with the Soviet Union was ended by concessions from Moscow; Belgrade was not obliged to give anything in return.

The *rapprochement* between Tito and Khrushchev in 1961 coincided with a return to the tight economic controls abandoned earlier in the year, attacks by Tito on 'rotten liberalism' in the arts and culture, and the re-imprisonment of Milovan Djilas for publishing his book *Conversations with Stalin*. But to assume a causal connection is, as Duncan Wilson says, 'to make too tidy a pattern out of the chaotic variety of events' [195 *p. 135*]. There was in any case a rapid reversal of policy in 1963: liberal economic reforms were instituted and a pluralistic, decentralizing constitution was adopted. Yugoslavia's economic connection with the West, so essential to her survival in the early 1950s, was not abandoned after the reconciliation with the Soviet Union. United States aid to Yugoslavia continued to play a vital economic role. Between 1962 and 1967 Yugoslavia received $536 million from the USA [188 *p. 271*]. Imports from the West rose from 29.7 per cent of the total in 1960–62 to 69.3 per cent in 1969–71. Exports to the West, in contrast, did not rise as a proportion of the total, owing to the opening of the CMEA market to Yugoslav goods after 1955 [188 *p. 273*].

At the Eighth LCY Congress in December 1964 Tito came down firmly in favour of further economic reform, decentralization and self-management. The solution of the national question, he said, was for the peoples of Yugoslavia to 'enrich each other by mutual cultural influences'; the national cultures of all the peoples would be encouraged to flourish freely [195 pp. 152–4]. Decentralization was applied, not just to the economy (by the Economic Reform of 1965) but to the LCY itself (its Central Committee was abolished in 1969 and it was, in effect, divided into eight sections, each section representing a republic or autonomous province). Neither under Khrushchev nor under Brezhnev did the Soviet Union attempt to induce Yugoslavia to alter its policies in these areas [36 p. 191].

## THE YEARS OF CONSOLIDATION

If we turn now to the second feature of the period, consolidation, we find there is a striking degree of uniformity underlying the divergences outlined in the previous section. This was partly determined by international factors. The Hungarian uprising and its suppression had important repercussions for the other nations of Eastern Europe, not just the Hungarians. It gave the Soviet leaders a severe jolt and made them decide to reaffirm their authority wherever possible. This reduced the room for manoeuvre enjoyed by all East Europeans. It also inspired local communist elites with fear of the people's anger; they could not forget that communists (mainly secret policemen, it is true) had been done to death in Budapest in November 1956. They therefore felt in need of Soviet protection. Finally, the West's lack of reaction to the bloody suppression of the uprising made it clear that the East Europeans were on their own. They could not hope to achieve genuine national sovereignty (apart from Yugoslavia, which already had it).

So a period of consolidation and stability ensued for Eastern Europe. Politically, the party oligarchies continued to rule almost without challenge, almost always under a single named leader, as in Stalin's time. But this was not a simple restoration of the system of Stalinism. By the end of the 1960s such a thing was impossible. The new way of ruling and organizing East European society was far less totalitarian than the old. The communist parties abandoned their aspiration to control the whole of society; instead they drew a sharp line between the private sphere, where the citizen was free, within the law, to seek his or her own advantage, and the public sphere, where the party's monopoly was fiercely defended. Non-participation in the rituals of socialism was now not punishable, although it was obviously not a recipe for social advancement. The purges had ended, but the organs of state security continued to watch carefully over society and punish dissent where they thought it necessary. Generally it was unnecessary. Instead of resistance, the pattern of the 1960s was sullen acceptance. This did not mean legitimacy. What Fehér and Heller say of Hungary can be applied more generally: 'János Kádár's enlightened police state was firmly consolidated but not legitimised' [144 *p. ix*]. The distinction is encapsulated by the striking concept of the 'niche society', examined in detail for the GDR by Mary Fulbrook [134 *p. 129*]. Outside working hours citizens were permitted to withdraw into a 'private niche' with which the state would not interfere. This made the absence of freedom more tolerable.

The East European economies continued to make good progress after 1956. The road to 'socialism' was pursued through a succession of Five Year Plans. Now more attention was paid to the needs of consumers: real wages rose substantially over the period 1956 to 1970. The average per annum increase varied from a high of 5.3 per cent (Romania) to a low of 2.8 per cent (Poland). The resulting decline in the rate of investment did not prevent economic growth from continuing at a rapid pace. The average annual rise in Net Material Product for the Eastern European members of the CMEA was 7.1 per cent in 1956–60, 5.3 per cent in 1961–65 (this reflected the impact of the economic crisis of the early 1960s) and 7.7 per cent in 1966–70. Even when scaled down by Western analysts these rates of increase come out at roughly 5 per cent per annum over the period [36 *pp. 200–1*].

This economic transformation had important social consequences, which reinforced trends that had already started during the Stalin era. More and more people left the countryside (by 1970 the urban proportion of the population was 73.8 per cent in the GDR, 62.3 per cent in Czechoslovakia, 52.3 per cent in Poland, 53.0 per cent in Bulgaria, 48.9 per cent in Hungary, 40.9 per cent in Romania, 40.2 per cent in Yugoslavia and 33.5 per cent in Albania), and the contribution of agriculture to national income continued to decrease (by 1970 it was 12.9 per cent in the GDR, 10.2 per cent in Czechoslovakia, 17.3 per cent in Poland, 22.6 per cent in Bulgaria, 17.8 per cent in Hungary, 19.1 per cent in Romania, 18.3 per cent in Yugoslavia and 34.5 per cent in Albania) [98 *p. 109*]. Conversely, the relative weight of industry increased progressively (these official figures are admittedly biased upwards by the irrational price structure that prevailed): between 1950 and 1970 the share of industry and construction in national income rose from 43.4 per cent to 57.8 per cent in Bulgaria, from 71.2 per cent to 73.5 per cent in Czechoslovakia, from 53.1 per cent to 69.1 per cent in the GDR, from 55.4 per cent to 55.6 per cent in Hungary, from 45.0 per cent to 67.3 per cent in Poland, and from 49.6 per cent to 70.9 per cent in Romania [72 *pp. 278–9*]. Roughly corresponding figures for Yugoslavia are 25.1 per cent in 1947 and 44.3 per cent in 1966 [194 *p. 246*].

The growth of industry had its counterpart on the land in the return of collective farming to the top of the agenda. Everywhere except in Poland and Yugoslavia a resumption of collectivization followed the suppression of the Hungarian revolt. This second attempt to destroy private farming was

1. Sceptical East German workers listen to Fritz Selbmann, GDR Minister of
Heavy Industry, opening a coke and lignite works, 31 August 1955.

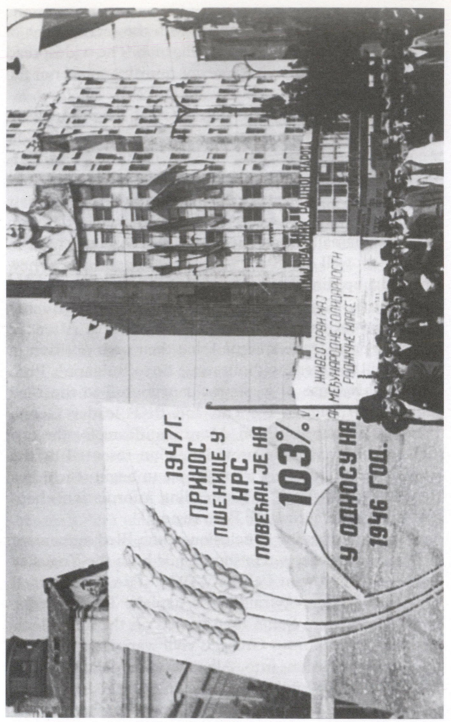

2. Communists demonstrate in Belgrade promising the doubling of wheat production in 1947, dominated by Tito's picture.

3. The female student militia on parade in Tirana, 1964.

4a. Tito, in discussion with his two chief lieutenants, Eduard Kardelj and Aleksander Ranković, at some time during the mid-1960s.

4b. A New Year's Eve Party in Yugoslavia at the end of 1967, attended by Tito and his wife Javanka. Tito (though a Croat by ethnic origin) is wearing Serbian national costume for the occasion.

5. The resurgence of protest in Poland: a student demonstration in Warsaw, March 1968.

6. Alexander Dubček acknowledges the crowd's enthusiasm for 'socialism with a human face'. Prague, May Day 1968.

7. Walter Ulbricht, the East German leader, visited Czechoslovakia on 12 August 1968. Here he is pictured presumably laying down the law to Dubček about the risks entailed in his reform programme.

remarkably successful, given that the efforts of the early 1950s had come up against strong peasant resistance. This time everything went smoothly. Why was this? For one thing, the resistance of the peasantry had already been broken in the first wave of collectivization. The last traces of armed peasant resistance were liquidated in 1958 (in the hills of Romania). Moreover, by the 1960s the peasantry were everywhere a declining class; the expansion of the industrial economy gave them for the first time the choice between staying and moving to town to take industrial employment. By 1960 the abolition of private property in the land was well-nigh complete. The proportion of land held in state and collective farms was 85 per cent in Albania, 91 per cent in Bulgaria, 87 per cent in Czechoslovakia, 84 per cent in East Germany, 77 per cent in Hungary, and 84 per cent in Romania [36 *p. 202*]. In Poland and Yugoslavia the extensive state farms set up in the early 1950s continued to exist (they covered 11.5 per cent and 9.4 per cent of agricultural land respectively) though collective farms were now practically non-existent (1 per cent of the land in each case) [81 *p. 80*].

In pushing forward collectivization the authorities were hoping to achieve economies of scale. The new collective farms were merged in the course of the 1960s and 1970s into much larger units. In Bulgaria, for example, the land had been consolidated into 957 gigantic collective farms by 1960. A decade later these had been replaced by 161 'agro-industrial complexes' [108 *pp. 149, 207*]. They were also provided with more equipment. In Eastern Europe as a whole, the number of tractors more than doubled between 1958 and 1968, to 11.6 tractors per 1,000 hectares of land. Yugoslavia alone failed to mechanize its agriculture at this time. There the number of tractors per 1,000 hectares was still only 3.4 in 1968 [72 *p. 380*].

One question which arose, once collectivization had been completed, was the status of the private plots collective farm employees were allowed to hold. Czechoslovakia followed the Soviet policy of severe restriction; Bulgaria and Hungary were more liberal. The latter approach paid off. In Bulgaria, 10 per cent of collectivized cultivated land had been leased back to peasant households by 1970; these private plots played a considerable economic role, producing 27 per cent of the country's meat and 26 per cent of its milk [106 *p. 208*]. In Hungary, 40 per cent of the income received by collective farmers in 1975 was derived from their private plots [81 *p. 157*].

Collectivization was associated with a reduction in the agricultural labour force. The rate of decline was spectacular. During the 1960s the annual percentage fall in agricultural employment was 2.5 per cent in Czechoslovakia, 2.9 per cent in Hungary and Bulgaria, 3.4 per cent in the GDR and 0.9 per cent in Poland (the decline in Poland was in reality faster than this, since 27 per cent of all peasant families derived most of their income from non-agricultural activities) [165 *p. 285*]. As we have seen, the urban proportion of the population increased by leaps and bounds. Millions of peasants moved to the towns and became industrial workers or entered the service sector.

The quiet years of consolidation that followed 1956 were interrupted twice: first by economics, then by politics. The crisis of 1960–62, which affected all the more advanced East European economies, added acuteness to the discussions around economic reform. A distinction began to be made, particularly in Czechoslovakia, where the crisis was felt most sharply, between extensive and intensive development. It was argued that until roughly 1960, extensive, purely quantitative development had been a rational economic strategy. There were existing raw materials that could be exploited; there were reserves of human labour that could be drawn into industry, released from the land by a collectivized and mechanized agriculture. Now that was no longer possible. The task of extensive development was complete, at least in East Central Europe. Further development would have to be intensive; gains could only be made by more efficient use of resources. An increase in efficiency could only be secured by the introduction of market mechanisms. The plan would remain, but would be combined with the market. After 1962 a start was made in several countries with reforms of this kind. Their key elements were: a reduction in the number of centrally planned output targets (under the Czechoslovak reform of 1967 the number of planned targets fell from 1,300 to 62); a greater emphasis on profit as a criterion of economic efficiency; a strengthening of economic incentives, with managers and workers receiving more money in more efficient enterprises; a partial liberalization of prices; and finally some decentralization of economic decision-making [36 *p. 107*]. There were limitations everywhere on the consistency with which these elements were introduced. Price reform, for instance, meant the freeing of a proportion of prices, excluding articles of everyday consumption. Under the Hungarian reform of 1968, 29 per cent of wholesale prices were freed. But decentralization was usually countered by the simultaneous creation of gigantic associations of enterprises. By 1970 the number of industrial enterprises had shrunk to 100 in Czechoslovakia, 90 in the GDR.

Another aspect of economic reform was the establishment of stronger economic relations with the West. This was the only way the Eastern economies could procure advanced technology; it was also a way of securing much needed capital. These factors operated far more strongly in the subsequent period, but the move away from bloc autarchy was already happening in the 1960s. This was less a matter of quantity (since the share of the West in Eastern European trade turnover remained static at 20 per cent) than of quality, since the West's restrictions on advanced technology exports, imposed at the height of the Cold War, were made much milder after 1960 [81 *p. 117*].

Whether a regime decided to pursue economic reform or not tended to depend on two things: its perception of the effectiveness of the existing economic system and the degree of independence it had towards internal pressure groups whose interests would be damaged by reforms. In Poland, for instance, the wide-ranging discussions of 1956 and 1957 about economic reform had no practical effect. There was a reversion after 1959 to tried and tested methods, with an increase in the number of obligatory targets from six to nineteen, a sharp rise in the rate of investment and a static level of real wages. In Romania there was no incentive to reform because the performance of the command economy in the 1960s was extremely good. Here the method of extensive growth, based on an increase in the input of resources and labour, continued to be effective. Romania was rich in natural resources (including sources of energy) and had an abundant supply of labour owing to the high birth rate. In Bulgaria, economic performance was also good, although here a shortage of labour began to develop owing to a severe decline in the birth rate (from 25.2 per 1,000 in 1950 to 16.3 per 1,000 in 1970) and the exhaustion of the rural population reserve. So there was some degree of economic reform after 1964, but it was limited to small-scale experiments in applying the profit criterion to individual enterprises.

All of this did not amount to much. None of the proposed reforms met the deeper problem of the lack of a rational price structure and the low level of productivity. They were also sabotaged by the bureaucracy. Over most of Eastern Europe the economic crisis of the early 1960s passed by without generating more than token reforms, with the possible exception of Hungary, where a New Economic Mechanism was introduced on 1 January 1968. This fairly promising reform was allowed to run for four years but was then cancelled by the Central Committee, which re-imposed controls on incomes, prices and foreign trade and returned fifty-one large enterprises to direct ministerial control in November 1972. The view that was taken within the party leadership was that the crisis was simply a blip in the system, not the sign of a deeper malaise; and this seemed to be justified by the continuously favourable figures of the remainder of the decade. It should be noted that the economies of several countries benefited from favourable terms of trade and cheap energy supplies from the Soviet Union, which gave ever-increasing hidden subsidies to its allies in the course of the 1960s. By 1970 the Soviet subsidy amounted to the equivalent of $2,589 million, $1,165 million of which went to the GDR (Bulgaria and Romania received nothing). At the time, however, this was known only to a few economic specialists.

In one country, the crisis of the early 1960s set off a much more general questioning of the system within the ruling party and among the population at large. This deserves to be examined in more detail, because the development of events eventually drew in the whole Soviet bloc.

## CZECHOSLOVAKIA IN 1968: THE LAST CHANCE TO REFORM

In Czechoslovakia reform was long overdue by the 1960s. As we have seen, the shock of de-Stalinization was overcome fairly easily by the new Czechoslovak communist leader Novotný, who stayed firmly in control of the party until 1967. Novotný's hold on the situation was however progressively weakened during the 1960s by a number of forces. The first was the evident stagnation of the economy. National income growth, which had hovered around a respectable 7 per cent per annum since 1953, suddenly plunged to 1 per cent in 1962; in 1963 national income fell by 2 per cent. The Third Five Year Plan had to be scrapped as its targets had become unrealistic. The economist Ota Šik responded to the challenge in 1964 by producing a reform proposal which envisaged enterprise autonomy, the abolition of obligatory targets and the physical allocation of supplies, and the freeing of some prices. These reforms remained on paper, however. Novotný publicly expressed his determination to resist any 'liberalizing influences' in the economy [62 *p. 187*]. In addition, the situation seemed to lose its urgency when it appeared that the country had weathered the crisis of the early 1960s and the upward curve of growth had resumed.

When an economic reform was finally implemented (January 1967) it was, in the reformers' view, prevented from taking proper effect by the resistance of conservative party officials. They concluded that political change and economic change were bound up together. Not only was political change needed to allow effective economic reform; economic reforms would react back on politics, creating, as the economic theorist Radoslav Selucký said, 'the basis for a pluralistic political system', although still within the socialist framework [81 *p. 212*].

So there was pressure from the reforming economists, and from those party administrators who agreed with them. There were two further forces at work. One was the discontent of the intelligentsia. The intellectuals had now cast off the shackles of fear and loyalty that bound them in the 1950s. They demanded the abolition of censorship and a thorough investigation and exposure of the crimes of the Stalin era. They did more than make demands. They went ahead with a considerable number of projects which were ultimately subversive of the current regime [117]. The mid-1960s were a golden age for Czechoslovak theatre, literature, cinema and social philosophy. At the same time the country's historians were quietly proceeding with their investigation of the Stalinist past. None of these activities was underground; their open existence testifies to the growth of a reforming faction within the CPCz itself.

One other force that weakened Novotný's hold on power needs to be mentioned. It was by no means the least important one. This was the sense of grievance felt by Slovaks at the failure of the communist party to live up to the promises of autonomy made in 1945. Slovakia had actually made tremendous economic and cultural progress in the intervening period, narrowing the historic gap which separated it from the Czech lands, but this did not divert the Slovaks (including the Slovak communist leaders) from their main demand for a genuinely federal state in which both nations would have complete equality of rights. Moreover, the purges of the Stalin era were often directed against Slovak communists like Vlado Clementis and Gustáv Husák, and the survivors demanded a thorough rehabilitation of the victims. When Alexander Dubček took over the Slovak communist party, in 1963, a man was in place who could forge an alliance between the national demands of Slovaks and the liberal aspirations of the intelligentsia as a whole.

The factional conflict within the communist party over these issues reached its height in 1967. Moreover, now the creative artists began to defy the party. Having in practice won the battle over artistic censorship, they turned to the broader political arena. At the Fourth Congress of the Czechoslovak Writers' Union, in June 1967, bitter battles were waged, and fiery speeches were made, about issues of both domestic and international politics. Leading writers such as Ludvík Vaculík and Ivan Klíma were expelled from the party as a result, and the proceedings were not published, but the half-hearted character of the repression was apparent from the absence of any more severe sanctions. The ferment continued. Eventually Novotný was overthrown, in January 1968, and replaced by Dubček as party leader, despite his attempt to call in the aid of the Soviet Union. The man in charge in Moscow, Leonid Brezhnev, probably regarded Dubček as an acceptable replacement [131 *p. 179*]. Thus began the 'Prague Spring' of 1968.

Dubček and his colleagues intended to reform communism, not to get rid of it. They issued an Action Programme of reforms in April 1968, which was actually a fairly moderate document [*Doc. 24*]. It covered all the areas where discontent had been growing since 1956: the role of the communist party, the position of the non-communists, the rights of the individual, economic policy and relations between Czechs and Slovaks. Moderate solutions were proposed in all areas, except one: the rights of the individual. The Programme envisaged freedom of assembly, expression and association; there would no longer be any preliminary censorship. The state security organs would not intervene in internal political matters. Moreover, the policy of the government reflected this. Dubček and his supporters wanted to encourage spontaneous action from below; he was confident that this would lead to a more humane socialism not a collapse of the whole system [131 *pp. 217–21*].

Others were not so sure. Communist leaders outside Czechoslovakia, from Brezhnev downwards, were extremely concerned about these developments. Warning after warning was given. The first indication of concern was the emergency session of communist leaders which met at Dresden on 23 March. Dubček reported on this to the April Plenum of the CPCz, but it was clear that he attached little importance to the concerns expressed. In his view, Czechoslovakia's allies 'accepted her line with understanding' and respected her 'sovereignty' as regards 'internal development' [131 *p. 208*]. The real situation was that Brezhnev was unwilling to intervene, but was under constant pressure from his East German and Polish partners, who were both extremely hostile to what was happening in Czechoslovakia. During the summer the conservatives were placed increasingly on the defensive there, and the view from outside was that the position of the CPCz itself was under threat.

The publication of the 'Two Thousand Words' Manifesto on 27 June was a decisive turning-point. It called on the people to force out party leaders who had abused positions of power by various forms of direct action, including 'demonstrations, strikes and boycotts' and threatened that the people would fight against 'foreign forces intervening in our development' by all means, 'if necessary with arms' [36 *p. 128*]. This brought a swift response from the Soviet leader. 'We cannot remain indifferent to the fate of socialism in another country', he said on 3 July. Shortly afterwards he invited the Czechoslovak leaders to a conference of all the Warsaw Pact states. The Dubček leadership feared rightly that this would be less a conference than a session at which they would be given a humiliating dressing down. Dubček advised against attending, and the Presidium of the party concurred with this (12 July). Five Warsaw Pact members accordingly met in Moscow on 15 July without Czechoslovakia (and without Romania, which also refused to attend). Ulbricht and Gomułka took the lead in pressing for strong action. A warning was issued that the alleged 'collapse of communist authority' would not be tolerated, and would meet with resistance from 'healthy forces' within the country. In carrying out this resistance, the 'healthy forces' would receive the aid of the 'parties of the fraternal socialist countries' [36 *p. 130*]. The Czechoslovaks replied (18 July) by denying that there was any 'threat to the socialist system or the political role of the CPCz', and asserting that, on the contrary, the decisions of the May Plenum (which had suspended the party membership of Novotný and many of his associates, and set 9 September as the date for an extraordinary party congress) had led to 'a rise in the authority of the new democratic policy of the party'. Instead of a meeting of all the Warsaw Pact allies, which would be based on 'one-sided information', Prague called for bilateral discussions, particularly with the Soviet leadership [131 *p. 291*].

Brezhnev accepted this suggestion, and Czechoslovak–Soviet talks accordingly started on 29 July at the Slovak village of Čierna nad Tisou. After this a broader meeting was held at Bratislava. The Bratislava conference issued a joint declaration on 3 August in favour of the development of 'fraternal cooperation' between the socialist countries, which was ambiguous enough to allow the CPCz leaders and much of Czechoslovak public opinion to hail it as a victory. It was a fateful error. Far from carrying out the measures called for at Čierna the Dubček leadership continued its course as if nothing had happened. A report on the general political situation, which the conservatives Alois Indra and Drahomír Kolder wanted the Presidium to discuss urgently, was placed at the bottom of the agenda, and the measures they proposed were rejected on 20 August. Shortly afterwards, during the night of 20–21 August, an invasion of the country was mounted by Soviet troops, assisted by small Polish, East German, Bulgarian and Hungarian contingents.

One question about 1968 which will probably remain unanswered, given that it relates to the psychology and character of the communist participants in the Prague Spring, is why Dubček and his supporters felt that they could defy the Soviet Union with impunity. As Kádár said to the Czechoslovak leader on 17 August 1968, four days before the invasion: 'Do you really not know the kind of people you are dealing with?' [13 *p. 157*].

One answer was given later by Edward Goldstücker, one of the more radical members of the CPCz leadership:

> We committed an error in 1968. Khrushchev's fall meant re-Stalinization and the evidence was there for everyone to read. ... Why were we misled? Because in Czechoslovakia the process had been delayed until 1963, so in 1968 we were out of phase with what was happening in Moscow. We were caught in the trough of the wave. [58 *pp. 73–4*]

Certainly Dubček himself was astonished when he heard the news of the invasion by the Soviet Union and its Warsaw Pact allies on 21 August. He thought that he, and the communist party, had retained sufficient control of the situation in Czechoslovakia not to be accused of allowing anti-socialist forces to get the upper hand. But the nature of the reform process initiated by the Action Programme of April 1968 was that it encouraged the spontaneous action of society; the Dubček leadership always refused to take the harsh measures that would have been needed to keep this within acceptable bounds. And, just as in Hungary in 1956, when they were able to rely on János Kádár, the Soviet leaders had the support of a faction within the party which would welcome their intervention. The letter of invitation to Brezhnev, which was kept secret for twenty-five years, finally surfaced in 1992 when President Yeltsin handed it to his Czechoslovak counterpart, President Havel. It was signed by the following five members of the Politbureau of the CPCz: Vasil Bil'ak, Antonín Kapek, Alois Indra, Drahomír Kolder and Oldřich Švestka. It called for Soviet aid 'to free Czechoslovakia from the threat of counter-revolution' [*Doc. 27*].

With the letter of invitation in their pockets, the Soviet leaders could hope to install an alternative leadership after the invasion, and indeed they did eventually succeed in this. But there was an unexpected interlude. The Czechoslovak people, far from being grateful, engaged in a well-nigh unanimous display of passive resistance in the week that followed, under the general slogan 'Not even water for the occupiers'. The Fourteenth Party Congress of the CPCz met secretly in a Prague factory and voted to continue the process of reform and throw all the conservatives off the Central Committee. Dubček had explicitly ruled out the use of force in his broadcast condemning the invasion. But the strength of passive resistance, combined with the refusal of President Svoboda to countenance the appointment of a government of the type set up in Hungary after 1956, compelled Brezhnev to fall back temporarily on Dubček and his colleagues, who had been kidnapped and flown to Moscow immediately after the invasion. They for their part were prepared to meet the Soviet leaders halfway. They signed the Moscow Agreement of 27 August, which preserved some aspects of the Prague Spring, but made the withdrawal of Soviet troops conditional on the 'normalization of the situation'. The Moscow Agreement required the re-imposition of party control over the mass media, including the dismissal of those who had allowed freedom of expression, a ban on political parties outside the National Front, the abrogation of the decisions of the Fourteenth Party Congress and the removal from office of certain specific persons regarded as a danger to socialism. The occupation would only be ended when 'the threat to socialism in Czechoslovakia and to the security of the countries of the socialist community' had disappeared [18 *p. 382*; 131 *p. 801*].

Whether a better agreement could have been secured has been a controversial question ever since. In any case, the requirement for 'normalization' was so vague that the Soviet side could use it to impose the complete reversal of the reforms of 1968. This happened gradually over the next year. It was a slow process. For one thing, Czechoslovak society itself continued to resist. One surprising aspect of this was the part played by the industrial workers. Before the occupation they had showed little interest in the reforms, which did not in fact offer them much. But now both unofficial Workers' Councils, which emerged after the invasion, and the official trade unions, waged a series of campaigns against the 'normalization' process. When the students went on strike in November 1968 there was a spontaneous work stoppage in solidarity with them. The Czech Metal Workers' Union threatened to strike against the dismissal of Smrkovský, the most radical member of Dubček's post-August team. And the official trade unions, previously a mere 'transmission belt' for party directives, proclaimed in March 1969 that they would never again accept subordination to the party [36 *p. 137*].

But the pressure of the occupiers was too strong. Dubček resisted every step of the way, but was gradually forced to jettison all of his liberal political colleagues, and eventually the Action Programme itself. He was eventually brought down by the 'ice hockey crisis' of March 1969, which demonstrated very clearly that the situation was by no means 'normalized' in the sense intended by the Soviet Union. Czechoslovak demonstrators responded to the news of their team's victories over the Soviet ice hockey team by going on a rampage against Soviet property in Prague. Dubček was accused of failing to maintain order. In April 1969 he was forced to resign his position. Gustáv Husák took over as First Secretary of the CPCz. The new party Presidium, elected at the same time, included none of the 1968 reformers except Dubček himself. The latter was in turn forced out in September. Over the next year Czechoslovak society was forced back to the situation of the early 1960s. The CPCz was purged of all those who had played any part in the events of 1968 or refused to disavow them. In order to survive the purging process, wrote Milan Šimečka, one of its victims, one had to lack 'independence of mind, generosity, tolerance, education, moral principles and courage' [129 p. 41].

The suppression of the Prague Spring in 1968 was a turning-point for Eastern Europe. From the rulers' point of view it indicated the danger of pursuing even a moderate reform; everywhere after 1968 one sees the screws being tightened again. Economic reform is abandoned, hesitant steps towards political liberalization are put into reverse. In the GDR it happened in 1968 (the end of the New Economic System); in Hungary in 1972 (the CC resolution condemning the operation of the economic reform); in Poland in 1968 (the suppression of the student movement and the purges of Jews and liberals from the media and cultural life); in Romania in 1971 (the start of Ceauşescu's 'cultural revolution' against liberal intellectuals and technocrats).

The impact of 1968 on attitudes in unofficial circles was even more profound. After 1968 all hope for reform within the communist framework died and dissident movements with more far-reaching objectives started to emerge. Their activities would eventually lead to the complete abolition of the Eastern European communist regimes. The contrast between before and after has been well put by János Kis, the Hungarian social critic: 'In the 1950s and 1960s you had the idea of reforms generated from above and supported from below; but after 1968 there was a new idea: meaningful change could only come through people's organizing themselves outside the structures of the party and the state' [24 p. 174]. This new strategy was adopted and implemented where possible during the 1970s and 1980s; ultimately it was to prove effective, in combination with the progressive decline of the East European economies and the revolution in Soviet thinking under Mikhail Gorbachev.

# PART THREE    ASSESSMENT

# CHAPTER SEVEN

# ACHIEVEMENTS AND FAILURES

In this section we shall endeavour to assess the balance of failure and success in the first twenty years of the communists' drive to transform Eastern European society and establish a new, more humane and progressive social order. We shall examine various areas where they endeavoured to do this: equality of social structure, improvements in the situation of women, access of all to education, health care, standard of living and general economic performance. We conclude by referring briefly to some of the leading historical controversies.

## EQUALITY AND INEQUALITY

Let us look first at egalitarianism. In theory the communists were committed to equality. As we saw in Chapter 4, a deliberate attempt was made in the 1950s to extend educational opportunities to the new 'ruling class', the proletariat. The Polish sociologist Alexander Matejko commented: 'The peasants and workers have risen to the foreground and gained access to education, including higher education; they have ousted the higher levels of society' [84 p. 63]. During the Stalinist period the former workers and peasants were often able to push the former middle classes out of managerial and technical positions. In Poland, for instance, by 1952 70 per cent of enterprise directors were of working-class or peasant social origin [166 p. 187]. In Hungary, by 1960 40 per cent of professional and managerial staff were of working class, 26 per cent of peasant origin [72 p. 317]. This was not the whole story. Despite the intentions of the ruling establishment the old intelligentsia managed to survive in the cultural field. In Poland, for instance, the creative intelligentsia 'retained most of its prewar characteristics'. The proportion of intellectuals of non-manual social origin was 60 per cent in 1967 [166 pp. 159–60].

Once the big Stalin-induced effort of the early 1950s had run its course, a new class, combining those who had risen up the scale and those who had held on to their position, was able to entrench itself socially. The class system now solidified. Class became hereditary again. Egalitarianism, enforced between 1948 and 1953, went into decline. In Czechoslovakia, the distribution of earnings in industry was at its most equal in 1954; thereafter the differential between technical staff and workers widened, so that by 1967 it had reached 25 per cent [127 *p. 128*]. Ideologically, egalitarianism continued to be upheld; but even here there were exceptions. Those who wanted to reform the communist system in the 1960s identified egalitarianism as one of its main failings. The 1968 Action Programme of the CPCz was explicit on this point: 'Levelling has spread to an unheard of extent. It places shoddy workers, idlers and irresponsible people at an advantage over those who are skilled; it advantages backward people as compared to those who respond to incentives' [18 *p. 97*]. In Hungary, too, reformers who supported the New Economic Mechanism in 1970 argued in favour of rewarding excellence: 'There is a top and meritorious elite which has grown up under socialism and is doing far more for society than the others. It deserves to enjoy a special financial status and to live in the style of the former ruling class' [150 *p. 365*].

There were admittedly some cases where an infusion of new blood took place, for specific reasons. Occasionally losses of cadres required fresh recruitment efforts, as in Czechoslovakia after the purges of 1969; in Poland after the fall of the Stalinists in 1956, and Gomułka's supporters in 1970; in East Germany in the 1960s to replace those who had emigrated to the West before the building of the Berlin Wall. But the general picture was one of blocked social mobility [82 *pp. 185–6*].

There was a permanent change in one area of social life: equality between the sexes. It might, however, be more accurate to speak rather of an equalization of the burdens of life and work. The formal position of the communists in favour of sexual equality was clear: the Czechoslovak Constitution of 1960, for instance, proclaimed that the 'equal status of women should be secured by the development of facilities and services which will enable women to participate fully in the life of society' [74 *p. 137*]. But did this happen?

The researches of Alina Heitlinger have illuminated this subject. The female participation rate in work increased dramatically: in 1950 it was 54 per cent, in 1960 71 per cent, in 1970 85 per cent. The number of pre-school nurseries increased from 4,932 in 1948 to 9,095 in 1964. The number of female pupils in secondary schools increased by 114 per cent between 1954 and 1965, while the number of male pupils only grew by 14 per cent. These educational opportunities, and a readiness to appoint women, meant that by 1970 almost half the employed specialists with higher education were female. But all these advances had not in fact improved women's status. The ratio of female to male income, which was 65 to 100 in 1946, was roughly the same (67 to 100) in 1970. The proportion of women in leading managerial positions remained static throughout at 5 per cent. The occupations that were open to women, such as teaching and medicine, tended to lose status for that reason. Moreover, having come home from a hard day's work, in an inferior position, for a lower salary, a woman then spent an average of 5 hours 42 minutes a day on housework [74 *pp. 140–55*]. Husbands refused to share in work regarded as undignified. This 'double burden' was made worse by the absence of labour-saving appliances. Moreover, politics remained a male preserve. Studies of other countries have confirmed Heitlinger's results [102 *p. 24*].

One way of improving women's situation and reducing the burden they bore was by giving them the opportunity to control the size of their families. In the first decade of communist rule, dominated as it was by the Stalinist legacy, family limitation was exceedingly difficult. Contraception, although not illegal, was not in widespread use, and the other answer, abortion, was illegal in Poland and Romania until 1956, in Czechoslovakia until 1957, in Yugoslavia until 1960, and in East Germany until 1965 (the practice enjoyed a short period of legality there between 1947 and 1950). Partly owing to these obstacles, increases in the birth rate were registered up to 1954 in most of Eastern Europe. The exceptions were Czechoslovakia and Bulgaria.

In the mid-1950s the birth rate began to fall dramatically everywhere (in Albania and East Germany the fall was delayed until the 1960s). This was a veritable demographic revolution. In Poland, the birth rate fell so far that it changed from being twice the British level in 1952 to below it in 1965. The legalization of abortion played some part in this decline, though Malcolm Potts argues that illegal abortions were already commonplace in the early 1950s and that the change in the law made little difference [90 *p. 243*]. The standard method of birth control continued to be *coitus interruptus* (it was used by 67 per cent of couples in Hungary in 1965, 64 per cent in Czechoslovakia in 1961 and 60 per cent in Slovenia in 1963). The inadequacy of the method meant the women frequently had to resort to abortion. Information on this subject is patchy, but we know that in Czechoslovakia in 1970 only 6 per cent of women used modern methods of contraception. Once abortion was legalized, rates climbed to remarkable levels, overtaking live births in Czechoslovakia, Hungary and Bulgaria by 1969. In Romania it was worse: in 1965 there were four abortions for every live birth [72 *p. 370*; 74 *p. 184*].

Faced with the prospect of an ageing population, or even a population decline, the authorities took fright, and introduced pro-natalist policies of various kinds [85]. Abortion was made harder to procure (except in Yugoslavia where it remained freely available). It was completely prohibited in Romania in 1966, restricted in Bulgaria and Czechoslovakia in 1972, in East Germany in 1968, and in Hungary in 1974. Positive incentives to have children were also introduced. Maternity leave was extended and family allowances were increased. Press campaigns stressed the importance of women's role as mothers and child-rearers. Government policies had a considerable impact on the birth rate almost everywhere. In the late 1950s and early 1960s, when governments took no positive measures, birth rates fell. In the late 1960s birth rates rose, as a result of prohibitions on abortion and incentives to motherhood [*Doc. 29*].

## EDUCATIONAL PROGRESS

The first and most basic task of any modern educational system is to bring about mass literacy. The East European communists succeeded in this, though in many cases they were building on the prior achievements of the prewar regimes. The rate of illiteracy was already low in East Central Europe on the eve of the communist takeover. In 1937 it was 3 per cent in Czechoslovakia, 7 per cent in Hungary and 18.5 per cent in Poland. In contrast, there was a long way to go in Yugoslavia (39 per cent), Bulgaria (29 per cent), Romania (42 per cent) and Albania (60 per cent). Progress was slow at first. By 1950 average illiteracy for East Central Europe was 5.9 per cent (excluding East Germany, where it was 1.5 per cent); for the South East it was still 25 per cent [73 *p. 216*; 79 *p. 358*]. But in the 1950s, thanks to universal education at the primary level, supplemented by adult education courses, most of South Eastern Europe also learned to read. Even in Albania illiteracy was down to 7.6 per cent by 1954.

The next task was to expand secondary education. Here the results by 1970 were patchy. Certainly there had been increases everywhere, but even so less than 50 per cent of the relevant age group were enrolled in secondary schools in Albania, Czechoslovakia, Poland and Romania, and nowhere in Eastern Europe did the proportion exceed 70 per cent. Access to higher education was even more limited. Here, enrolment by 1970 was between 10 and 15 per cent of the age group (in Hungary it was lower, at 6.8 per cent). The highest enrolment level was in Yugoslavia (14.6 per cent) [72 *p. 246*]. Initially the student body was weighted towards the sons and daughters of workers and peasants: in Poland the proportion of working-class origin rose from 7 per cent in 1946–47 to 38 per cent in 1951–52, while the proportion of peasant origin rose from 4 per cent to 24 per cent. The proportion with professional parents fell correspondingly. This was a result of the quota system for entry. In 1960 it was abandoned; the results were immediate. The proportion of students of working-class origin fell to 26 per cent, of peasant origin to 18 per cent in 1960–61. For the next ten years these proportions remained static. In Poland, it has been said, higher education was and continued to be 'a means of self-reproduction of the intelligentsia' [82 *pp. 385, 399*; 166 *p. 21*]. In Czechoslovakia, too, an attempt was made in the Stalin era to alter the class composition of the student body: between 1948 and 1959 the proportion of students of working-class and peasant origin rose from 18 per cent to 41.5 per cent in the Czech lands [115 *p. 309*]. The figures remained roughly constant in the 1960s, but there was a substantial increase between 1970–71 and 1972–73 (from 32 per cent working class to 45 per cent working class in Czechoslovakia as a whole) which reflected a deliberate return to class-based entrance policies during the process of 'normalization' which followed the upheaval of 1968. The verdict of most observers is that, with this temporary exception, and also the exception of East Germany, where students of worker or peasant background occupied 58 per cent of the university places in 1958–59, the communists' efforts to wipe out educational inequality of opportunity were unsuccessful [82 *p. 386;* 115].

## HEALTH

Dramatic improvements in health care took place in all Eastern European countries in the first two decades of communist rule. It would be possible to give figures on the number of hospital beds, doctors, dentists and nurses. They all show remarkable increases by 1970, and in most cases more favourable proportions than some Western European countries [72 *p. 371*]. But the most dramatic way of illustrating this is to look at the results. Infant mortality fell, the length of the average person's life rose. These are two separate phenomena, not necessarily linked. A comparison with two representative non-communist countries, West Germany for East Central Europe, Greece for South Eastern Europe, shows that the improvements in this period were in almost every case as dramatic as they were in the West [*Docs 30, 31*].

The early years of communism thus saw a considerable degree of convergence between Western and Eastern Europe in standards of health. By the mid-1960s the East–West differential between age-standardized mortality rates was less than 3 per cent for males, 8 per cent for females. Life expectancy at age 1 for both men and women was roughly the same everywhere in Europe. The East had pretty well caught up with the West in this respect. The length of the average male life after age 1 was 69–70 years. For females it was 73–74 years [69 *p. 348*]. Unfortunately, the story does not end there. The subsequent period, the final decades of communist rule, from the mid-1960s to the end of the 1980s and beyond, saw a decline in male life expectancy at age 1 in Eastern Europe, although female life expectancy registered a slight increase [87 *p. 201*]. Meanwhile, Western life expectancy was racing ahead. The gap between the East and the West widened once again.

## STANDARD OF LIVING

Taking the period as a whole there was undoubted progress in the standard of living. The communists were committed to improving the quality of life for the mass of the people, though of course this commitment was limited, firstly, by the stress on the long-term character of this goal (in the short term the main aim was to create a modern industrial economy), secondly, by the Cold War with its associated military imperatives and, thirdly, by the way in which the quality of life was defined (in purely material terms). It is true to say that the standard of living continuously improved in the years after the death of Stalin in 1953. The average diet became more nourishing, with a progressive shift away from cereals and potatoes to meat, milk and sugar. Average daily calorie consumption in Eastern Europe was over 3,000 (except in Albania where the average was 2,400) in the late 1960s. This compares well with the West. The proportion of meat within this was around 30 per cent in East Central Europe, while in the South East it was closer to 15 per cent [72 *p. 381*]. High-quality consumer goods, however, were not so readily available. Even so, considerable progress was made in many areas in the 1960s. In East Central Europe the proportion of households with television sets rose from an average of 5 per cent in 1960 to 22 per cent in 1970; the proportion with radio receivers was constant at 25 per cent. The motor car was another matter. Here there was a clear difference between Czechoslovakia and East Germany, which managed to raise car ownership from infinitesimal levels in 1960 to 5.7 per cent and 7.2 per cent respectively in 1970, and the rest of the region, where progress was slight (Yugoslavia did best, reaching 3.5 per cent by 1970). There were, finally, distinct improvements in the housing situation, from a rather low starting level [*Doc. 32*].

## ECONOMIC PERFORMANCE

One disadvantage the East European economies faced in their endeavour to match Western performance lies in the Cold War itself. Not only did it distort their development by compelling a one-sided emphasis on products of military significance; the West did its best to limit their access to advanced technology, through a Coordinating Committee set up in 1950 to enforce a trade embargo against the Eastern bloc countries [94 *pp. 446–50*].

Another problem, according to some observers, lay in the nature of the planning process. It seemed to be impossible to make sure that appropriate quantities of all commodities were produced. The economic analysts János Kornai and Jan Winiecki have pointed out that this was a system that generated excess demand, at one pole, and systematic shortage, at the other [83; 101]. The result was, as the Polish joke had it, that 'in a planned economy you ended up trying to assemble ten bicycles with nine screws' [55 *p. 181*].

Nevertheless, if we compare the record of the East European economies in the 1950s and 1960s with that of the United Kingdom, a representative Western economy, we find a tremendous improvement in their relative positions. This of course does not disprove the theoretical arguments of Kornai and Winiecki about the economy of shortage, but it does show the effectiveness of the methods of the command economy in the short term and under appropriate conditions.

Some necessarily tentative calculations of changes in GDP were made by economists attached to the European Economic Commission in 1969 [*Doc. 33*]. There is much controversy about the degree of reliance to be placed on official figures. Jan Winiecki estimated in 1986 that the Eastern European growth statistics for 1950 to 1973 were inflated by a proportion ranging from 9.4 per cent (Hungary) to 44.4 per cent (East Germany) [*100 p. 343*]. Even if we take this into account, the economic gap between East and West had still closed considerably by 1969. Derek Aldcroft has described this achievement as 'little short of a miracle' [*60 p. 183*].

The populations of Eastern Europe could now be sure that they would be fed and clothed. What they did not have was product quality, availability (the notorious queues) or choice. In the 1960s this situation began to improve, not so much through government action as through the rise of the so-called 'second economy' or 'shadow economy', a complex of semi-legal and illegal spare-time economic activities grudgingly tolerated by the regimes [*92 pp. 120–36*].

The failure of the communist economic system was not clearly evident until the 1980s; but there were already signs of a slower growth rate in the 1970s. As we have seen, economists and party leaders, aware of the defects of the system, endeavoured from 1956 onwards, by fits and starts, to institute economic reforms. There was a reform spurt in Poland in 1956; in Czechoslovakia in 1959; in the GDR in 1963; in Hungary in 1965; in Poland again in 1966; in Czechoslovakia again in 1967. The Romanians, Bulgarians and Albanians did not feel it was necessary to make any serious changes as their economies were still delivering rapid output growth in the 1960s. Elsewhere the jury was still out on the effectiveness of the economic reforms. Later on, in the 1980s, the views of economists and economic historians became more definite: Brus's 1989 verdict was that with the single exception of Hungary attempts at economic reform had failed in Eastern Europe [*64 p. 62*]. János Kornai concurred, adding however that the reform process in Hungary could not go any further without going beyond the limits of the socialist system [*33 p. 86*].

Another aspect of Eastern economic growth, not brought out by these global figures, was the equalization of regions. The only place where this did not take place was Yugoslavia, because of the Yugoslav move towards a market-based economy. Even there strenuous attempts were made to overcome the imbalance between the more developed north and the less developed south. They were, however, not entirely successful. In 1962 national income per head in Yugoslavia ranged from 195 per cent of the Yugoslav average in Slovenia down to 69 per cent in Macedonia and 37 per cent in Kosovo-Metohija. Communist League leaders in the less developed areas protested bitterly against the failure of the central authorities to reduce these disparities in development and income [181 *p. 34;* 195 *p. 142*]. But the general picture in Eastern Europe was that formerly agrarian regions became industrialized, with a corresponding fall in income differences. Slovakia's relative income was 60 per cent of the Czech level in 1948; by 1988 it was 87 per cent.

The final picture, then, is mixed. The standard of living had increased for most people. Their health had improved. They were better housed and better provided with material goods. They were unable, however, to take charge of their own lives, and they never really accepted the system that had been imposed on them after 1948. Even so, although by the 1960s many inhabitants of Eastern Europe were dissatisfied, and increasingly aware that their rulers were offering them less than people had in the West, there was little active dissidence. The golden age of dissidence is the 1970s and 1980s. What dissidence there was before 1968 within Eastern Europe was also somewhat conservative in its objectives. It did not question the basic ideological pillars of the system. The turning-point was the crushing of the Prague Spring. After that, not only did a far more active opposition movement develop, at least in East Central Europe, it now aimed to destroy communist rule at its roots.

## THE BALANCE SHEET OF HISTORY

Evaluations of the period of communist rule in Eastern Europe, whether by historians or political scientists, have been overwhelmingly negative in the West. Since 1989 the Eastern Europeans themselves have largely adopted this verdict. There is, therefore, a broad historiographical consensus about the overall picture of communist rule. There are, however, many disagreements on specific points. For example, some writers have identified certain key turning-points, explicitly or implicitly, when an initially promising development was snuffed out. There are also those who reject this approach completely, saying that the system was irredeemably flawed from the outset. It was much easier to take the latter view after the 1960s, when it was clearly apparent to all that the Soviet system was stagnating, particularly in its Eastern European version [29 *p. 512;* 101; 157].

Turning-points that have been put forward include 1948 (the end of socialist independence and the suffocation of the workers' control movement) [114]; 1956 (the suppression of the Hungarian revolution, which it is argued was about to open the path to a 'third way' to socialism based on the ideas of István Bibó [144; 151]; 1968 (the suppression of Czechoslovakia's experiment in 'socialism with a human face') [13; 118]; and the late 1960s (exhaustion of attempts to implement economic reforms within the system and the end of the period of continuous improvement in health and life-expectancy) [63; 69].

The subject has also been studied by sociologists and political scientists. Stress here is on the functioning of communist rule in Eastern Europe, and its response to the nature and requirements of modern industrial societies in general. Ken Jowitt has written on 'revolutionary breakthroughs' and the 'mobilization' of society (generalizing from the example of Romania) [176]; Charles Gati on communist rule as a process of 'modernization' [72]. More recently, Jan Gross and Andrew Janos have taken the opposite line and stressed the traditionalism of the system, examining the continuities between pre-1939 nationalist, wartime Nazi and post-war communist experiments in controlling the economies and societies of the region [51; 40]. There is also a wide range of literature on the communist economic system as applied to Eastern Europe [62; 64; 83; 88; 93; 94; 101; 103]. The social history of the region, in contrast, was long neglected, and only came into its own recently, with studies on equality and inequality [67; 82], social change [72; 84; 87; 127; 166] and the position of women [74; 75; 89; 102].

The international context, Eastern Europe's relations with the Soviet Union, has always been a favoured subject for Western historians and analysts. This question is still in flux, even now, given that hitherto secret documents, made available after 1991, have by no means all been fully exploited in the current historical literature. Extracts from some of them are included in Part Four of this book. So far the new documents have, above all, shed light in a number of dark corners, such as the Prague coup of February 1948, Khrushchev's decision to mount the second invasion of Hungary in 1956, and Brezhnev's decision, along with his Warsaw Pact allies, to attack Czechoslovakia in 1968. The new evidence has by no means settled the controversies on these issues conclusively. For instance, Stalin's views and intentions towards Eastern Europe after 1945 have long been the subject of debate. Did he intend all along to impose a system of communist rule? Or was he only driven in this direction by an apparent increase in threats from the West after 1946 (as Vojtech Mastny has recently concluded, having examined the latest evidence) [45 *pp. 20–5*]?

We can therefore look forward to continued historical controversy about communist Eastern Europe. It is hoped that the extracts from documents given below will give the student some insight into the basis for these controversies as well as a feeling of the flavour of a period, and of a social and governmental system, which now belongs to history, since it is unlikely ever to be resuscitated.

The documents in this section, in many cases not previously available in English, are chosen for the light they throw on decision-making at the top of the communist hierarchy. East Central Europe is better represented here than South Eastern Europe. This is because it is only in Poland, Hungary, Germany and former Czechoslovakia that a start has been made with the publication of the communist archives. Some translations from Russian sources have been included because of the light they throw on the general context of communist rule, and particularly on Stalin's approach to Eastern Europe.

*The Yugoslav version of the National Front, the AVNOJ, was set up in November 1942. This is the main resolution passed at its second meeting, in November 1943. The claim that it was the legal government of Yugoslavia at first infuriated Stalin, as it cut across his international policy, but a year later both he and his Western allies accepted the claim, calling only for the addition of some representatives of the London government.*

The Anti-Fascist Council of the People's Liberation of Yugoslavia (AVNOJ), as the highest and the sole genuine representative of the will of all the peoples of Yugoslavia, resolves:

1 To constitute itself as the supreme legislative and executive representative body of Yugoslavia, as the supreme representative of the sovereignty of the peoples and the state of Yugoslavia as a whole, and to establish a National Committee of the Liberation of Yugoslavia as an organ with all the characteristics of a peoples' government, through which the AVNOJ will exercise its executive function.
2 To deprive the traitor exile 'government' of Yugoslavia of all the rights of a legitimate government of Yugoslavia and in particular of the right to represent the peoples of Yugoslavia anywhere and before anyone.
3 To examine all the international agreements made abroad in the name of Yugoslavia by the exile 'government' with a view to their annulment or their renewal, and not to recognise any agreements the so-called 'government' may sign in the future.
4 To build Yugoslavia on democratic, federal principles as a state community of peoples with equal rights.

Declaration of the Second Session of the Anti-Fascist Council of the People's Liberation of Yugoslavia (AVNOJ), held at Jajce, Yugoslavia, 29 November 1943.

*Prvo i Drugo Zasedanje AVNOJa*, Prosveta, Belgrade, 1983, p. 288.

*This speech was made at the second session of AVNOJ. Tito combines two themes: an insistence on sole power in Yugoslavia, with the London government to have no share in it at all, and a measure of reassurance to both Stalin and the West that he and his supporters do not intend to establish a communist system. This was untrue, but everyone turned a blind eye to the falsehood because of the tremendous role of the Yugoslav partisans in tying down the Nazi forces militarily.*

We are very well aware that the traitor-government is doing all it can to smuggle itself back to Yugoslavia at any cost (and that goes for the king too) before the people utter their decisive word on their future. We know that certain reactionary circles abroad are helping that government. But we also know that the vast majority of progressive democratic elements in the Allied countries sincerely desire our people to decide their future for themselves. ...

We have been slandered from all sides. ... All the occupiers and traitors ... say that our people's liberation struggle in Yugoslavia is a purely communist affair, involving the bolshevization of the country, an attempt by the communists to seize power, the abolition of private property, the destruction of the church and of religion, the destruction of culture and so on. ... Very few people believe these lies any longer, and least of all the peoples of Yugoslavia. ... The times are past when a handful of reactionaries could ascribe such matters to the communists of Yugoslavia, in order to isolate them from the people.

Bearing this in mind, ... it is essential to take steps to ensure that our peoples obtain a state system based on the brotherhood and equality of rights of all the peoples of Yugoslavia and which would guarantee genuine liberty and democracy to all sections of the community. The monarchy has completely discredited itself in the eyes of the people during the last twenty three years. The evidence for this has been proved hundreds of thousands of times and all our peoples know it. Only a republican form of government can ensure that such disasters never again come upon our people.

H.M. Christman (ed.), *The Essential Tito*, David and Charles, Newton Abbott, 1971, pp. 24–6.

<br>

DOCUMENT 3   **LETTER FROM MOSCOW TO POLISH COMMUNISTS IN THE HOMELAND, 18 JULY 1944**

*This document shows the contrast between the home-grown radicalism of the local Polish communists and the moderate 'National Front' policy favoured by Moscow. The programme of the KRN, set up in December 1943, was too radical for Moscow, involving as it did the nationalization of industry and the expropriation of all large landed estates.*

The day of decision for the Polish question is approaching. It is becoming clear that the government will consist of an enlarged National Council of the Homeland (KRN). The success of this government rests on two conditions: (1) it must be a truly national government supported by the majority of the people; (2) it must pursue policies conducive to understanding between the

Allied nations in the Teheran spirit. Both conditions will be met only if there is a sustained and consistent national front policy. ... But the party is being inconsistent in its campaign for a national front. For example, the platform of the nationalization of industry cannot be construed as an attempt to split the reactionaries or win over floating opinion. ... Moreover, land distribution among agricultural workers drives a wedge between us and the peasants. ... The effect of these policies would be the abandonment of efforts to win over the majority of the people. ... This has to be avoided at all costs. The correct policy for a national front requires a series of concessions and compromises which will split our opponents without fundamentally altering our aims. ... We realize that our left-wing opponents are making irresponsible promises which might cause us trouble. Nevertheless we must not be diverted from fundamentals, from the creation of a national front.

Letter from the Central Bureau of Polish Communists in the USSR to the Central Committee of the Polish Workers' Party, Moscow, 18 July 1944.

> A. Polonsky, and B. Drukier, *The Beginnings of Communist Rule in Poland*, Routledge and Kegan Paul, 1980, Document 17, pp. 230–2.

---

**DOCUMENT 4   MINUTES OF THE 14 DECEMBER 1944 MEETING OF THE POLITBUREAU OF THE CENTRAL COMMITTEE OF THE POLISH WORKERS' PARTY. TOP SECRET. THREE COPIES MADE**

*The subject under discussion here is the Polish Socialist Party (PPS) and how to deal with it. Ultimately it was absorbed into the Polish Workers' Party (PPR). But in the meantime it was essential to cooperate with it, as the PPR was not a strong force in Polish society. The PPS could provide a mass base, provided that it was kept under control. Hence the arguments here about the relative reliability of its leaders.*

The following were present: Gomułka, Bierut, Minc, Berman, Werbłowski and Radkiewicz.

Comrade Tomasz (Bierut) reported on his visit to Moscow: immediately after my arrival I was summoned to Bulganin, with whom I then proceeded to Stalin. At that time a meeting of the Politbureau was being held in the Kremlin. Stalin received me in a very friendly way, showing interest above all in the question of agrarian reform and the current situation in the PPS. He was very satisfied with the course of the agrarian reform. I presented the situation in the PPS to Stalin under the aspect of two currents pervading that party, namely the sincerely democratic current represented by Morawski, and the WRN* current, the spokesman of which is Drobner. The following conversation took place about Morawski:

Stalin: How is Morawski holding up in the PKWN? Tomasz: He is cooperating with us sincerely. ... Stalin: What do you think of Morawski? Tomasz: He is a young man, inexperienced, but full of good will. He stands sincerely on the ground of cooperation with the Soviet Union. Stalin: Was Morawski generally known as a political activist before the war? Tomasz: No. He worked in the cooperative movement. Stalin: And who was known? Tomasz: Dubois and Barlicki, but they died at the hands of the Germans. Stalin: What kind of influence has Morawski in the PPS? Tomasz: Dominant influence, greater than Drobner. Stalin: What is Morawski's attitude to the PPR? Tomasz: Good in general, there is nothing one can reproach him with. Stalin: If that is so, then Morawski will in future be a communist. Tomasz: I share your opinion. ...

Later on Stalin returned once more to the question of the PPS. They all started to put pressure on Morawski, and Stalin proposed the removal of Drobner from the committee [the PKWN]. Morawski defended Drobner, to which Bierut replied that Drobner was however a long way away from us ideologically. Stalin commented that all parties had divided during the war on the question of relations with fascism, and Morawski would not be able to count on cooperation between the Londoners and the PPS. ... On the way to their vehicles after the visit Morawski exploded at Bierut, saying: 'You have bandits and Pilsudski-ites in your ranks. Purge yourselves, and not our party.' There was an unpleasant exchange of words between them, and Bierut departed without saying goodbye to Morawski.

A. Garlicki, *Z Tajnych Archiwów*, Polska Oficyna Wydawnicza 'BGW', Warsaw, 1993, pp. 10–14.

DOCUMENT 5   **THE CZECHOSLOVAK GOVERNMENT PROGRAMME OF 21 MARCH 1945 (THE KOŠICE PROGRAMME)**

*The programme of the Czechoslovak coalition government, drawn up by the communist leader Gottwald, accepted by all other parties at the end of March, and made public in April 1945, was a fairly moderate document, making no reference to the nationalization of industry or to socialism. Its strongly nationalist tone, directed against Germans and Hungarians, expressed the agreed views of most Czechs and Slovaks. The Slovaks' own claims to equality and autonomy were also largely recognized here.*

1   The new government is the government of the broad National Front of Czechs and Slovaks and is constituted by representatives of all social strata and political tendencies which have conducted a national liberation

struggle to overthrow German and Hungarian tyranny. The National Front government will put in hand as soon as possible after liberation universal, secret and direct elections to the Constituent Assembly.

2  The government will support with all means possible the advance of the Red Army. On liberated land all citizens of Czechoslovakia capable of bearing arms will be mobilized for this task. In the enemy's rear the government will organize a partisan struggle against the occupation. ...

4  Czechoslovak foreign policy will be based on the closest possible cooperation with the victorious Slav Great Power to the East, the Soviet Union. Practical cooperation with the Soviet Union will be implemented in all spheres – military, political, economic and cultural.

5  In domestic policy the basic principle will be that the people are the source of all state power. In place of the former bureaucratic administration, new organs of public authority will be set up, namely elected National Committees. The government will implement its policies through the National Committees.

6  Recognizing that the Slovaks must rule in their Slovak lands, just as the Czechs must in their national patrimony, and that the republic will be re-founded as the joint state of the Czechs and Slovaks, enjoying equal rights, the government will incorporate this recognition in the appropriate political measures. Joint state affairs will be administered by the central government in the closest cooperation with the Slovak National Council. ...

8  Czechoslovak citizens of German and Hungarian nationality who had citizenship before 1938 will have their citizenship confirmed if they fought against the German Nazis and Hungarian irredentists. Other Czechoslovak citizens of German and Hungarian nationality will lose their citizenship. ...

10  The property of Germans and Hungarians who assisted the occupiers will be confiscated and placed under state administration, as will the property of Czechoslovaks who betrayed the nation.

11  The government approves the confiscation of the land of enemies and traitors carried out by the Slovak National Council and its division among small farmers, and proposes to extend the practice to the whole country, giving preference to people who served in the national liberation struggle as partisans.

12  The government will support the private initiative of entrepreneurs, craftsmen and other producers.

M. Klimeš, P. Lesjuk, I. Malá and V. Prečan (eds), *Cesta ke Květnu*, Nakladatelství ČSAV, Prague, 1965, Document 130, pp. 380–90.

*This document relates to the discussions in the Central Committee of the Polish Workers' Party (PPR) over the adoption of a milder policy towards the opposition. This fitted in both with the agreement subsequently reached between Stalin and the West at the Potsdam Conference of July 1945 over the entry of some London Poles into the Lublin government, which required some move towards compromise, and with the growing sense of isolation felt by the Polish communist leaders themselves because of popular resistance provoked by the harsh measures they had been carrying out since October 1944. Hence the attacks on 'sectarianism'. Włodzimierz Zawadzki, attacked here by name, was a scapegoat for an agreed policy. He was soon expelled from the PPR (November 1945). Gomułka stressed in his speeches here that the change in policy of May 1945 did not represent a '180 degree turn'. In essentials the policy remained the same. But Soviet advisers were made less prominent, and an attempt was made to cut down on the assistance of the Red Army by building up a Polish internal security force (the KBW)\*.*

Extracts from Gomułka's speech:

We do not receive reports of the actual mood of the population. Either the facts are not ascertained at all or they are deliberately distorted. The present political situation in Poland contains many grave and dangerous elements – there are even features of a political crisis developing. Political stabilization is absent. We do not know how to achieve it, even though the other parties, which have until now oriented themselves towards London, are also in crisis. ...

Food riots are not directed against ... democratic Poland. The majority of the working class is in favour of the system as a whole, and the government. But there is wavering among a considerable part of the peasantry and the intellectuals. Some people advocate elections. But we would emerge weak and defeated from them because political stabilization has not taken place here. The agitation of the reactionaries over the 'Sovietization' of Poland has had a strong impact on the Polish mind. It affects a considerable part of the nation. It affects the mood of our allies in the coalition, especially the PPS, which is more independent.

Terrorist activity is increasing in extent and seriousness. Moreover, the enthusiastic attitude of society towards the Red Army has greatly fallen off. The prevalence of hooliganism and murders has contributed to this, but in this atmosphere there is a danger that the reproach of being a Soviet agency may take root, that we may become isolated. The masses ought to look upon us as a Polish party. Let them attack us as Polish communists, and not as Soviet agents.

I now come to our party's political line. ... A genuine and principled turn in the politics of the basic party organizations needs to be made. ... One sphere where sectarian errors have manifested themselves strongly is security. The security organs are starting to grow into a second government within our country. The organs conduct their own policy, in which one is not permitted to intervene. ... In Gdańsk they are proposing to burn Germans. ... This is the road to the political wilderness. If things continue in this way we shall become the worst sort of NKVD* agency. ... But if we isolate the reactionaries it will be easier for us to eliminate them physically. Liquidation by the security organs is needed, but it must be accompanied by a big consciousness-raising effort by the party.

Extracts from the Minutes of the meeting of the Central Committee of the PPR, held on 20–21 May 1945, published in A. Kochański (ed.), *Protokół obrad KC PPR w maju 1945 roku*, (Dokumenty do dziejów PRL. Zeszyt 1), Instytut Studiów politycznych PAN, Warsaw, 1992, pp. 13–16.

---

**DOCUMENT 7    STALIN'S ADVICE TO THE POLISH COMMUNISTS, 14 NOVEMBER 1945**

*This document underlines the readiness of the Polish communist leaders to consult Stalin on all matters, great and small. Stalin's answers to their questions show clearly that he did not envisage the immediate establishment of a Soviet-type system in Poland, and that he was keen to avoid giving the impression to the outside world that he did.*

Moscow, 14 November 1945. Secret.
To Comrade Molotov and the Group of Four [namely Beria, Malenkov, Mikoyan and Vyshinsky]

Stalin's Report on a discussion with Gomułka and Minc

No minutes were taken of the discussion, as the Poles did not consider it necessary. I am therefore informing you of the contents in question and answer form.
Question by the Poles: Should we adopt a law on the nationalization of large-scale industry and the banks?
Answer by Comrade Stalin: Now that Beneš has accepted a law of this kind in Czechoslovakia the time has come when its adoption in Poland too is necessary.
Question: Should the PPS's proposal for the abolition of grain procurements and the proclamation of a free market with unregulated prices be accepted?
Answer: This would not be a tragedy, as sooner or later the Poles will have to take these measures, since under a non-Soviet system and in the absence

of wartime conditions there is no possibility of retaining a system of grain procurement in the long run.

Question: Would I object if the Poles accepted an American or British loan?

Answer: A loan can be accepted, but without any conditions limiting Poland's freedom to make use of it ...

Question: Should representatives of the Soviet communist party be invited to the forthcoming PPR congress?

Answer: It would be better not to invite them, otherwise our opponents would be able to say that the PPR congress is taking place under the control of the Soviet communist party.

Question: May we proclaim at the congress that the PPR continues the line and the traditions of the Communist Party of Poland, which was liquidated just before the war?

Answer: No, since the Communist Party of Poland turned into an agency of the Piłsudski-ites. It would be better to say that the PPR is a new party entirely unconnected with the previous communist party.

Question: Morawski is not behaving well. If he does not straighten himself out in the immediate future we would like to replace him (as head of the government) with Mr. Lange, present Polish ambassador to the United States, a moderate PPS member, well disposed towards the communists. What do you advise?

Answer: If there is no other way, and if it impossible to appoint Bierut (the Poles think this is inappropriate) then you must have a go with Lange, and make use of him to break up the PPS.

The rest of the meeting was about the provision of seed-corn and railway transport. But you already know about those matters.

STALIN

[22], No. 112, pp. 301–2, 302–3.

DOCUMENT 8    THE CZECHOSLOVAK COMMUNIST LEADER KLEMENT GOTTWALD REPORTS A DISCUSSION WITH STALIN IN JULY 1946

*The period of relative moderation in communist policy between 1945 and 1947 is here given an ideological justification. The notion of different roads to socialism meant that a peaceful, parliamentary transition was possible. It fitted well with Czechoslovak experience up to that point.*

I talked to Stalin during my most recent stay in Moscow. Comrade Stalin told me that, as experience has demonstrated and the classics of Marxism-Leninism have taught, there is not just one road, through Soviets and the dictatorship of the proletariat. Under definite conditions there can be another road. In fact, after the defeat of Hitlerite Germany, after the Second World War, which on the one hand cost many victims but on the other hand tore the mask from the face of the ruling classes in many countries and raised the consciousness of the broad popular masses, many possibilities and roads opened for the socialist movement. As examples he indicated Yugoslavia, Bulgaria and Poland and described our country in so many words as a place where a specific road to socialism was possible.

[22], p. 579, footnote 3.

| DOCUMENT 9 | REPORT FROM THE POLISH COMMUNIST LEADER GOMUŁKA TO STALIN ON THE POLITICAL SITUATION IN HIS COUNTRY, 18 AUGUST 1946 |
| --- | --- |

*Gomułka reports here directly to Stalin on the main issue clouding relations between the PPS and the PPR in postwar Poland. The socialists were beginning to show a disturbing degree of independence, in particular a wish to maintain the multi-party system and to allow the Peasant Party (PSL)* * to continue existing as a genuine force in the country. Gomułka's response is to suggest 'forcible measures' against his coalition colleagues if they continue to be obstreperous.*

1. We consider that there is no possibility of creating a bloc with the PSL since the PSL will not agree to the offer of 25 per cent of the seats and we cannot offer more.
2. In these conditions it is necessary to go into the elections of January 1947 in a bloc without the PSL.
3. In connection with this, we must get the PPS to abandon its present policies of retreating in face of the PSL, attacking the PPR and badgering the state security organs, and instead to support the sharper course against the PSL (the course of keeping Mikołajczyk in the government while simultaneously applying on a broad scale measures to disband the PSL's local organizations).
4. If we cannot get the leadership of the PPS to abandon its present line there remain two perspectives: a) the removal of Osóbka-Morawski from the post of prime minister; b) a takeover by the left wing of the leadership of the PPS. This will turn out to be impossible, probably, without the application of some forcible measures.

Signed, on behalf of the Politbureau of the CC of the PPR: Wiesław. 17 August 1946.

[22], No. 168, p. 504.

| DOCUMENT 10 | GHEORGHIU-DEJ APPEALS TO STALIN OVER THE HEADS OF HIS PARTY COLLEAGUES, JANUARY 1947 |

*These two short extracts show Romanian communist leader Gheorghiu-Dej reporting secretly to Soviet envoy Vyshinsky on his colleagues, but getting into an embarrassing situation in Moscow over this.*

Extract One: From the Diary of A.Iu. Vyshinsky. Report of a meeting with Gheorghiu-Dej, 23 January 1947.

Dej asked his interpreter to leave and we were alone. He communicated the following: in the party he is constantly meeting obstacles to his work from Ana Pauker, [Vasile] Luca and in part Teohari [Georgescu]. It was not intrigues exactly, but it was Pauker and Luca's failure to recognize his authority as General Secretary of the party. The position of Pauker and Luca in the leadership undermined his authority. Complaints are to be heard that Romania is run by the Jew Pauker and the Hungarian Luca, and people say Pauker is an agent of Moscow. Measures should be taken to change this position, first and foremost against Pauker, who ought to be sent to work abroad, for example in Paris as representative of the International Federation of Women. This would bring an end to undesirable rumours and gossip.

Dej said that Pauker, Luca and others were opposed to the decision of the communists to take over the Ministry of the Economy. They said the economic situation was so grave that it would seem better to let other parties take responsibility for failure. Dej said on the contrary that solving the economic problem was so important that the communist party could not fail to take responsibility for this.

[22], No. 188, p. 559.

Extract Two: A report of a discussion with J.V. Stalin, 2 February 1947.

Stalin said that he had heard rumours that some people wanted the Romanian party to consist simply of Romanians, that is, speaking concretely, that Ana Pauker and Vasile Luca, who were not Romanian by nationality, would not be able to occupy leading positions. In this case the communist party would turn from a social, class party to being a racial party. If it retains its social character it will develop and get stronger, but if it acquires a racial character it will be unavoidably ruined. Dej replied that there were no currents in the Romanian communist party that maintained this. Stalin said that if that is indeed so, it is a good thing.

[22], No. 191, p. 565.

DOCUMENT 11    COMMENTS BY GÁBOR PÉTER, HEAD OF THE HUNGARIAN STATE SECURITY SERVICE, ON THE ORGANIZATION OF POLITICAL INVESTIGATIONS, APRIL 1947

*These chilling comments were made by the head of the Hungarian State Security Service (ÁVO) to an official of the Foreign Policy Section attached to the Central Committee of the Soviet communist party. It is rare indeed to find a direct admission by a secret policeman that his victims have been tortured. Yet here it is. The improved methods learned from visiting Soviet experts were slightly less unpleasant (involving sleep deprivation and psychological pressure) but more effective.*

Eighty per cent of the political police in Hungary are communists. Thus the organization is essentially in our hands. It is true that two assistant police chiefs belong to other parties, but we make sure that they don't get to know what they ought not to know. The majority of people in the police are newcomers. They lack experience and find the work difficult. We have learnt much from our Soviet comrades. General Belkin has given us a lot of help. Our main task is to achieve results without the application of physical force. It is impossible to say that everything is all right in this respect at present, but in comparison with the previous situation we have unquestionably made progress.

    We consider it our main task to find out everything as early as possible and to inform our leaders. With this goal in mind we have set up a widespread network of informants. We have our people in all the political parties. We have succeeded in winning over political activists from other parties. Recruitment takes place thanks to our possession of compromising materials. Fearing exposure, people start to cooperate with us. In the country districts, however, our network of informants is weak. But we have our people in all the ministries and all the churches. The political police give great assistance to the communist party. We have succeeded in finding out the intentions of our political opponents before inter-party discussions. We listen to all the most important telephone conversations between the prime minister and the party leaders, and report on them to Comrade Rákosi.

Record of a conversation between G.Ia. Korotkevich and G. Péter on the Organization of Political Investigations, at the beginning of April 1947. [22], No. 205, pp. 605–6.

**DOCUMENT 12    THE REJECTION OF THE MARSHALL PLAN BY CZECHOSLOVAKIA IN JULY 1947: A LETTER FROM KLEMENT GOTTWALD**

*The decision of the states of Eastern Europe not to take part in the Marshall Plan\* is often seen as a turning-point in international history and the real beginning of the Cold War. For Czechoslovakia it meant that the narrow limits of her independence were made plain. This letter shows that the decision was enforced by Stalin.*

To Mr. President (Beneš), Mr. Vice-Premier Široký and State Secretary Clementis

I was received twice by Generalissimo Stalin. The first time shortly after our arrival, the second time at 11 p. m. At the second visit the rest of the Czecho-slovak delegation was also present, and on the Soviet side Molotov. We mainly discussed participation at the Paris Conference (on the Marshall Plan). Stalin spoke first on the inquiries the Yugoslav, Polish and Romanian governments had made in Moscow before their decisions. Stalin and Molotov did not hide the fact that they were surprised by the decision of the Czechoslovak government to accept the invitation to Paris. They emphasised that in their view the direct aim of the Marshall Plan and the Paris Conference was to create a Western bloc and isolate the Soviet Union by offering the prospect of illusory credits, which the people who called this conference would be absolutely unable to provide. Even if perhaps in the future America might be able to provide credits this could not fail to exert significant influence on the political and economic independence of the recipients. In view of that situation, the Soviet Union considered our participation to be a breach in the front of the Slav states and an act directed against the USSR. Stalin proclaimed that what was at stake was our friendship with the USSR. There was no-one in the Soviet government who doubted our friendship with the USSR, but our participation at Paris would demonstrate in fact to the peoples of the USSR that we were allowing ourselves to be used as an instrument against the USSR, which neither Soviet public opinion nor the Soviet government could tolerate. We therefore ask you to call together all available members of the government and acquaint them with our conversations with Stalin and Molotov. We consider it essential to cancel our acceptance of the Paris invitation, and to make this public officially by 4 o'clock this afternoon. Apart from this, you must telephone us immediately to inform us of the decision.

*Signed*:    KLEMENT GOTTWALD (*Prime Minister of Czechoslovakia*)
JAN MASARYK (*Minister of Foreign Affairs*)

PROKOP DRTINA (*Minister of Justice*)
JIŘÍ KAŠPÁREK (*Czechoslovak Chargé d'Affaires in Moscow*)
Date: 10 July 1947

R. Jičín, K. Kaplan, K. Krátký and J. Šilar, (eds), *Československo a Marshallův plán. Sborník dokumentů*, (Sešity Ústava pro soudobé dějiny, vol. 1), Ústav pro soudobé dějiny ČSAV, Prague, 1992, Document 42, pp. 57–8.

## DOCUMENT 13   RECORD OF SOVIET–BULGARIAN–YUGOSLAV DISCUSSIONS IN MOSCOW, 10 FEBRUARY 1948

*Stalin shows here his realism about international politics, and his readiness to abandon the Greek communists. Stalin also severely criticized both the Yugoslavs and the Bulgarians at this meeting. It is clear that Stalin was beginning to think that no compromise with Tito was possible. The word 'not' in line three is evidently a mistake in transmission as it contradicts Stalin's next sentence, as well as the Yugoslav sources, such as M. Djilas, [2], p. 178.*

Stalin: Recently I have started to have doubts about the victory of the (Greek) partisans. If you are not convinced that the partisan movement will win, it will have to be folded up. The Americans and the English are [not] very interested in the Mediterranean. They want to have a base in Greece and will not be sparing of the means to maintain a government there which guarantees this. This is a big international question. If the partisan movement is brought to an end they will have no reason to attack you. It is not so easy to start wars now. ...
Kostov: We think the defeat of the partisan movement in Greece would create a very serious situation for the other Balkan countries.
Stalin: It goes without saying that the partisans should be supported. But the struggle should be postponed to a better time. ...
Kardelj: We think there are no essential differences between us. This is a matter of a few isolated mistakes.
Stalin: These are not isolated mistakes but a system.

A record taken by the Bulgarian communist Vasil Kolarov of this meeting, published in 'Na poroge pervogo raskola v "sotsialisticheskom lagere"', *Istoricheskii Arkhiv*, 4 (1997), pp. 99–101.

### DOCUMENT 14   GOMUŁKA WRITES TO STALIN EXPLAINING WHY HE CANNOT STAY IN THE POLISH PARTY LEADERSHIP, 14 DECEMBER 1948

*After explaining that he could not continue serving, first because the party insisted on a public confession at the August 1948 Plenum of errors he had only committed in closed party meetings and second, because the party allowed a slanderous campaign against him, he added a third reason: the excessive number of Jews in the party apparatus. Twenty years later, now back in power, he presided over a purge which removed most of the remaining Jews from the party (1968).*

All members of the Politbureau know my attitude to personnel policy in relation to Jewish comrades. I have stated this more than once. The personal composition of the leading organs of the state and party apparatus, viewed from the national point of view, creates an obstacle making the widening of our basis more difficult, especially among the intelligentsia, and also in the countryside and first and foremost among the working class. It is true that I too can be seen as responsible for such a high percentage of Jews in the leading state and party apparatus, but the main blame for this lies above all with the Jewish comrades. As General Secretary I did not find that they understood or supported my position on the personnel policy the party should conduct. On the contrary, their systematic practice proved that they did not share my point of view. The assertion that a serious shortage of Polish party cadres makes it impossible to carry out any other personnel policy than the present one is simply not true. Cadres will never develop if the party does not create the necessary conditions by promoting the most capable comrades to responsible positions.

On the basis of a series of observations, one can say quite definitely that a section of the Jewish comrades do not feel they are linked with the Polish nation, hence with the Polish working class, by any kind of bond. They take up a position which can be described as national nihilism. These facts have not been taken fully into account in the selection of candidates for various high positions.

I consider it necessary not only to stop any further increase in the proportion of Jews in the state and the party apparatus, but also gradually to reduce that proportion, particularly at the highest levels. To judge from my experience as General Secretary I am convinced that I could not take even the slightest step in this direction without coming up against all kinds of open or concealed machinations aimed at bringing to an end my activity in the party. If I were a member of the Politbureau I would not be able to view this question with indifference.

Vl. Gomułka,
Warsaw, 14 December 1948.

[22], No. 307, pp. 940–1.

DOCUMENT 15    RECORD OF GOMUŁKA'S INTERROGATION, 20 FEBRUARY 1952, BY GENERAL ROMAN ROMKOWSKI, DEPUTY MINISTER OF PUBLIC SECURITY

*This document throws some light on the methods of investigation used in Poland during the Stalinist period, and on Gomułka's defiant attitude. He was not physically tortured but he was held in isolation from his arrest in August 1951 onwards.*

R.: We have been authorized by the party leadership to conduct your interrogation.

G.: (*Interrupting*) Interrogation in connection with what? What are the charges against me?

R.: We shall talk about that in the course of the investigation, and the whole matter will be made clear.

G.: I don't know why you are behaving like this and so far no one has said anything to me about this.

R.: These questions will be clarified in the course of the investigation.

G.: Why was I arrested?

R.: I have the impression that the reasons why you find yourself in this position are not entirely unfamiliar to you. At the August (1948) Plenum you began a self-criticism. You promised the Party further statements in written and other forms explaining a whole series of questions. You are not doing that.

G.: (*Interrupting*) I want to clarify a certain matter. Are you talking to me on the instructions of the Party and as its representative, or as an official of the security service? ... By whom have you been authorized? ...

R.: I speak to you not only as a functionary of the security service but as a man whom the Party has authorized to conduct an investigation of you.

G.: In view of this, won't you have to tell me what I am accused of?

R.: But I have already told you, these questions will become clear in the course of the investigation. I started to tell you that at the August Plenum you promised the Party that you would clarify a whole series of questions. You promised to make a self-criticism.

G.: I did make a self-criticism and I have nothing more to add to it.

R.: Are you telling me you have nothing to say to the Party, to us in this case?

G.: That depends on what the question is.

R.: But we consider you owe us an answer on a whole range of matters in connection with your self-criticism. About the enemies of the Party, their place in our Party, where they sprang from, on whose behalf they are working, why they took up one position and not another during the

Occupation and after the Liberation. What do you have to tell us about these matters? ...

G.: I have nothing to tell you about this. I told the party leadership all I knew.

A. Garlicki, *Z Tajnych Archiwów*, Polska Oficyna Wydawnicza 'BGW', Warsaw, 1993, pp. 166–7, 168–9, 170.

---

**DOCUMENT 16   CRITICISMS BY THE SOVIET LEADERS OF THE POLICY OF THE SED IN EAST GERMANY AND INSTRUCTIONS ON HOW TO IMPROVE IT, JUNE 1953**

*The Soviet leaders did not mince their words in making these criticisms of the policies of the Stalin era in East Germany. They clearly regarded the hasty imposition of a socialist system there as a serious mistake. Some of the practical steps recommended here were taken, but many were not, because in the aftermath of the rising of 17 June 1953 it was decided that any further retreat was dangerous.*

An extremely unsatisfactory political and economic situation has arisen in the German Democratic Republic as a result of the implementation of an erroneous political line. There is serious discontent among the broad masses of the population. ... This is most clearly evident in the mass flight of the inhabitants of the GDR to West Germany. Between January 1951 and April 1953 447,000 people have fled to West Germany. ... This includes many members of the SED.

The main cause of this situation is the erroneous course adopted at the Second Conference of the SED [held in July 1952], and approved by the Soviet Politbureau, of an accelerated construction of socialism, in the absence of the real internal and external prerequisites needed for such a policy. ... The accelerated development of heavy industry, without a secure raw material base, the severe restriction of private initiative, which has damaged the interests of a broad stratum of small-scale proprietors in town and country, the precipitate creation of LPGs[*] without the necessary basis in the villages, have led to serious difficulties in supplying the population with industrial products and food, the ruin of a large number of small proprietors, artisans and traders and brought wide strata of the population into opposition to existing authority. Things have gone so far that over 500,000 hectares of land have been left uncultivated and the German peasants have begun to abandon their farms and move to West Germany...

All this creates serious dangers for the continued political existence of the GDR[*]. To improve the situation it is necessary to abandon the course towards forcing the construction of the socialism...

The following measures are to be recommended:

1 End the artificial promotion of the LPGs. All existing LPGs should be carefully checked and those without a voluntary basis are to be dissolved. ...

3 The policy of restricting and forcing out medium and small capital is to be rejected as premature. The economic life of the republic can only be restored by making use of private capital in small-scale industry, agriculture and commerce...

4 The Five Year Plan should be revised to slow down the present excessive tempo of development of heavy industry, and the production of mass consumption goods should be sharply increased. ...

6 Civil rights and legality should be strengthened, and severe punitive measures should not be used except in case of necessity.

R. Steininger, *Deutsche Geschichte seit 1945. Darstellung und Dokumente in vier Bänden.*
*Band 2: 1948–1955,* Fischer Taschenbuch Verlag, Frankfurt am Main, 1996, II, Document 34,
pp. 241–2, 243, 244, 245, 246.

DOCUMENT 17   REPORT OF IMRE NAGY TO THE CENTRAL COMMITTEE OF THE HWP ON 27 JUNE 1953

*Imre Nagy was a veteran Hungarian communist who was removed from office in 1949 because of his opposition to the policy of agricultural collectivization. He was appointed to replace Rákosi as head of the government in June 1953. The report he delivers here is a severe indictment of the policies of the previous five years. Like the party resolution that followed [Doc. 18] it did not surface until many years later.*

The actual direction of the party was not in the hands of its elected organs but was seized by Comrades Gerő, Farkas and Révai under the leadership of Comrade Rákosi. ... They seriously undermined the successful realization of the Communist principle of criticism and self-criticism. They regarded any criticism coming from below as representing the voice of the enemy, and they dealt with it as such. Instead of pointing out each other's mistakes, they defended each other from criticism, and they took even the slightest criticism as a personal insult. They regarded themselves as infallible. ...

Our state security organs have been responsible for a series of violations of legality committed primarily against the village population. The mistakes committed in this field, the violations of legality, shook the very foundation on which our state is based, the alliance of the workers and the peasantry. ... The task of the new government will be to introduce laws that will bring to an end the mistakes of the past, disband the internment camps and proclaim an amnesty. The problem of the internal deportees must be settled, and it must be made possible for them to choose where they wish to live. ...

Grave mistakes have been committed in our economic policies. The essence of the mistakes is that we failed to realize the basic economic law of socialism – the constant raising of the standard of living of the population. On the contrary, the attempt to achieve the maximum development of heavy industry, which in plain words was megalomania, was accompanied by a fall in the standard of living of the workers. ...

Serious mistakes have been made in the field of agriculture too. There was a general fall in agricultural production, and a neglect of the production of independent farms. In practice nothing was done for the independent farmers, despite the fact that the greater part of our agricultural production is provided by independent farms. ... Moreover, the party's 1948 policy of collectivizing agriculture within three or four years was incorrect. The exaggerated pace of collectivization inevitably led to violations of the voluntary principle, and the direct employment of economic or political force. The correct policy of controlling the kulaks was turned into a policy of liquidating them. This alone was a grave error. It led the peasantry to abandon production. This is clearly evident from the large growth of state reserves of uncultivated land.

*Labour Focus on Eastern Europe*, 8, 1 (summer 1985), pp. 6, 10, 11, 12.

DOCUMENT 18    THE HUNGARIAN WORKERS' PARTY RESOLUTION OF
28 JUNE 1953 CRITICIZING THE PREVIOUS PARTY REGIME

*This resolution, severely criticizing the Stalinist leaders of Hungary, was adopted on direct instructions from Moscow. It is similar in many ways to the instructions issued earlier in the month to the East Germans [Doc. 16]. At this stage changes could only take place in this way. One remarkable sidelight on the prevailing atmosphere in 1953 is the reference here to the dominant position of people of Jewish origin in the top leadership of the party. Although Rákosi had to accept the resolution itself, he was strong enough to prevent its publication. Amazingly, it remained secret until 1986.*

The Plenum of the Central Committee of the HWP declares that the party leadership, with Comrade Rákosi at the helm, has made serious mistakes in its political programme and practical work of the past years. These mistakes have had negative consequences for the living standard of the population in general and especially of the working class; they have weakened the relationship between the party and the working class and have in general negatively influenced the relationship between party, state and working masses.

Industrialization was regarded as an end in itself without considering the interests of the working class and working people. This forced development of heavy industry presupposed resources and raw materials that were in part just not available. Agricultural production was neglected and collectivization was pushed forward at far too rapid a tempo. Imre Nagy argued against this policy but the party leadership not only failed to accept his position but penalized him for it.

Mistakes in the party's general line and in economic policy contributed greatly to the application of administrative measures against workers, with the result that people were victimized by the police and the courts while enduring rough treatment by officials. From 1951 to 1 May 1953 the police imposed penalties in roughly 850,000 cases. Between 1950 and the second quarter of 1953, 650,000 cases came before the courts, with penalties imposed in 350,000 of them. The wholesale application of administrative measures has aroused ill feeling among workers and led the old intelligentsia into an attitude of resignation.

The State Defence Authority (ÁVH) has been inappropriately led by the party and personally by Comrade Rákosi. The cult of personality is also the rule in the military; in the army leadership this is coupled with the tendency to force the expansion of the military without regard to the economy. Comrade Farkas is chiefly responsible for this.

Instead of a collective leadership we have direction by one individual, and Comrade Rákosi is largely responsible for the associated cult of personality. The number of cadre positions held by leaders of Hungarian lineage is small, and the few who have attained high position often only have formal authority. Leadership is concentrated in fact in the hands of a foursome: Rákosi, Gerő, Farkas, and Révai.

G. Litván (ed.), *The Hungarian Revolution of 1956. Reform, Revolt and Repression,*
Longman, 1996, pp. 25–6.

| | |
|---|---|
| DOCUMENT 19 | **EXTRACTS FROM THE SIXTEEN DEMANDS OF THE STUDENTS OF THE BUDAPEST TECHNICAL CONSTRUCTION UNIVERSITY, 22 OCTOBER 1956** |

*These demands became in effect the programme of the Hungarian revolution of 1956. In calling for multi-party democratic elections, freedom of the press and the withdrawal of Soviet troops they went beyond what was acceptable either to Imre Nagy or to the opposition within the communist party; but the development of events in the subsequent week pushed Nagy towards adopting this programme as his own.*

1  We demand the immediate withdrawal from Hungary of all Soviet troops.

2  We demand elections by secret ballot to all the organs of the Hungarian Workers' Party. Once elected these organs must call a party congress at the earliest possible moment and elect a new central leadership.

3 The government must be reorganized under the direction of comrade Imre Nagy; all the criminal leaders of the Stalin–Rákosi era must immediately be removed.

4 We demand a public trial of Mihály Farkas and his accomplices. Mátyás Rákosi, the man responsible for the miserable situation of the country, must be brought back here and handed over to the judgment of the nation.

5 We demand the holding of elections by general, equal and secret ballot on a multi-party basis, to form a new National Assembly. We demand that the right to strike be guaranteed. ...

7 We demand the reorganization of the whole of Hungary's economic life, with the involvement of our own specialists.

8 We demand that the foreign trade agreements our country has signed be revealed, and real data on our reparations payments be produced; in addition, correct information must be given on the exploitation of our deposits of uranium ore, and on the Russian concessions. Hungary must have the right to dispose freely of its uranium ore at world market prices and for hard currency.

9 We insist on a full review of the existing work norms in industry, and the establishment of a minimum wage.

10 We demand that the system of obligatory agricultural deliveries be put on a new basis. We demand equal support for individual peasant farms.

11 We demand a review of all political and economic trials and the liberation and rehabilitation of those unjustly condemned ...

12 We demand freedom of opinion, of expression, of the press, and a free radio, and a new mass circulation newspaper for the MEFESZ* (Federation of Hungarian University and College Students' Associations). We demand access to our 'personal dossiers' and their liquidation.

13 We demand the immediate dismantling of the statue of Stalin, and the erection on the same spot of a memorial to the heroes and victims of the struggle for freedom in 1848–1849.[1] ...

15 We express our solidarity with the students and young people of Poland and Warsaw who are taking part in the movement towards Polish independence. ...

[1 The revolution of 1848 and the subsequent war of independence fought by the Hungarians against the Habsburg Monarchy is regarded as one of the most important events in Hungarian history. It was, however, ignored during the Stalin period, partly because of the embarrassing fact that Russian troops participated in the suppression of the rising in 1849.]

*Sovetskii Soiuz i Vengerskii Krizis 1956 Goda. Dokumenty*, Moscow, 1998, No. 75, pp. 316, 317, 318.

## DOCUMENT 20    THE POLES CONFRONT KHRUSHCHEV, OCTOBER 1956

*These extracts from the minutes of a session of the Politbureau of the Central Committee of the PZPR held on 19 October 1956 show how tense the situation was when the Soviet leaders arrived unannounced and uninvited with the intention of overawing the Polish communist leaders and dissuading them from making what they regarded as unacceptable concessions to the movement of reform that was sweeping the country.*

Comrade Gomułka informed the Politbureau about the meeting at the airport with the Soviet delegation. 'Talks like this I have never held with party comrades. It was beyond comprehension. How can you take such a tone and with such epithets turn on people who in good faith turned to you?' ... Khrushchev attacked Comrade Ochab for 'treacherous activities' and added 'this game won't work with us'. The entire discussion was carried on in a loud tone so that everyone at the airport heard it, even the chauffeurs. I replied: 'If you talk with a revolver on the table you don't have an even-handed discussion. I cannot continue under these conditions. We can listen to the complaints of the Soviet comrades, but if decisions are made under the threat of physical force, I am not up to it, as I am ill. I don't want to break off Polish–Soviet friendship. I believe what we propose will strengthen it. But any other resolution of these matters would only strengthen the anti-Soviet camp.'

*The meeting adjourned to allow Gomułka and fourteen other Polish delegates to meet the Soviet leaders for talks. No official minutes of these Polish–Soviet discussions of 19 October 1956 have been released. The Soviet copy is still in the closed section of the Presidential Archive in Moscow. But notes were taken by one of the Polish participants, Alexander Zawadzki, and the following passage comes from them.*

The Soviets complained of the abrupt removal from the Polish Politbureau of a group of comrades who are seen by the nation as supporters of friendship with the USSR. Mikoyan cited Gomułka's 1948 letter to Stalin complaining about 'the excessive number of Jews in high positions and the national nihilism that characterizes some Jewish comrades.' He (Mikoyan) considers it correct to decrease the congestion of Jews in the PZPR. Now Gomułka will be pulled to the top by the Jews and then they will drop him again. Economically we need nothing from Poland, he added. From 1959 we shall end our orders for coal from Poland.

L.W. Gluchowski, 'Poland, 1956. Khrushchev, Gomułka and the Polish October', *Bulletin*, Cold War International History Project, Washington, DC, 5 (Spring 1995), p. 40.

*The continuing uncertainty in the Soviet Presidium even after the return of
the Soviet delegation is shown by these extracts from the minutes of its
sessions of 20 and 21 October, and of the session of 24 October at which
some Eastern European leaders were present.*

20 October
Speaker not identified: The only way out – to finish with what is going on in
Poland. If Rokossovsky [Marshal K.K. Rokossovsky, a Soviet citizen of
Polish origin who was made Minister of Defence in 1949, but whose
removal was one of the main Polish demands] is left alone, then be patient
for a period of time. Manoeuvres. Prepare a document. Set up a committee.

21 October
Khrushchev: Bearing in mind the situation, we should renounce the idea of
armed intervention. Exercise patience. (All in agreement). A letter must be
sent to Gomułka about the KGB advisers. In relation to generals and officers
we shall ask him to prepare his proposals, and we shall agree to their recall.
The earlier we give up the Polish coal the better.

*Back in Moscow a few days later, Khrushchev announced the Soviet side's
concessions to a joint meeting of the Soviet Presidium and representatives
from the Czechoslovak, East German and Bulgarian parties (24 October
1956). It is notable that he continues to reject the views of the Poles but still
concedes their demands: the SED leader Walter Ulbricht, in contrast, continued to condemn the Poles uncompromisingly.*

Session of 24 October 1956
N.K. Khrushchev (CPSU): In Poland there have been many changes in top
party positions, defended by Gomułka on the ground that 'those removed
had lost the confidence of the party masses'. These Polish arguments are very
unpersuasive and seem to be outright fabrications. Moreover it is untrue
that Poland's obligation to deliver cheap coal to the Soviet Union has caused
the difficult economic situation there.

We think that in the case of Poland it is necessary to avoid nervousness
and haste. We must help the Polish comrades to straighten out the party line
and reinforce Polish–Soviet friendship. The USSR will most probably agree
to the Polish request for a loan.

Walter Ulbricht (SED): We approve the tactics of the CPSU towards
Poland, but condemn the Poles for opening doors to bourgeois ideology, for
drifting instead of leading, and for failing to clarify certain ideological
matters in advance.

Minutes of the Sessions of the Presidium of the Central Committee of the CPSU, held on 20 October, 21 October and 24 October 1956.

'SSSR i Pol'sha: Oktiabr' 1956-go', *Istoricheskii Arkhiv*, 1996, 5/6, nos 2, 4, and 8, pp. 182–7.

---

**DOCUMENT 22** **DECIDING WHAT TO DO ABOUT HUNGARY: MEETINGS OF THE SOVIET PRESIDIUM, 28 OCTOBER, 30 OCTOBER, 31 OCTOBER, 1 NOVEMBER 1956**

---

*It is evident from these notes, not revealed to the outside world until 1996, that the Soviet leaders approached the question of Hungary with great hesitation. There was even a moment, on 30 October 1956, when it looked as if the Soviet government was going to issue a declaration withdrawing its troops from Hungary, as a preparation to settling the crisis peacefully. In fact, they even envisaged withdrawing from the whole of Eastern Europe. Mikoyan, who was still in Budapest studying the situation, certainly favoured a peaceful settlement throughout, and he was extremely upset on his return on 1 November to find that a decision to intervene had been made in his absence. The reasons for the overnight change of views, between 30 and 31 October, were evidently both domestic and international.*

### 28 October 1956

Khrushchev: Things are getting more difficult. Demonstrations are reported. Kádár's attitude: engage in discussions with the centres of resistance. The workers are supporting the revolt...

Voroshilov: We are in a bad situation. We must work out our political line and bring in a group of Hungarian comrades. Mikoyan is not capable of doing this work. A group of comrades must be sent. We shall not withdraw our armed forces. It is necessary decisively to crush the rebellion.

Molotov: Things are going badly. The situation is worsening. ... We must agree on the limits within which we will permit a retreat. If they don't agree when we decide, then we go in with troops.

Khrushchev: We have very wide responsibilities. We must take account of the facts. The uprising has spread to the provinces. The army may go over to the rebels. ... Should we support the Nagy government? Yes, there is no other way...

### 30 October 1956

Khrushchev: Discussions with the Chinese leaders. Two paths. Military: occupation. Peaceful path: withdrawal of the army, discussions. Adopt a declaration today on the withdrawal of our forces. The whole Chinese Politbureau upholds this position.

## 31 October 1956

Khrushchev: The army should not be withdrawn from Hungary and from Budapest, and we must start an initiative to bring order to that country. Our party would not understand it if we gave Hungary to the imperialists as well as Egypt. If we leave Hungary it will encourage the American, English and French imperialists. They will see this as weakness on our part and go onto the offensive. We have no other choice. We went to meet the Hungarians halfway but now there is no government. Now we should set up a Provisional Revolutionary Government, headed by Kádár.

## 1 November 1956

Mikoyan: I am still opposed to the use of force. Let us wait 10 to 15 days, to see if the existing government can stabilise the situation. If that happens, everything will have turned out for the best...

> 'Kak reshalis' "voprosy Vengrii". Rabochie zapisi zasedanii Presidiuma TsK KPSS Iiul' – Noiabr' 1956g.', *Istoricheskii Arkhiv*, 1996, no. 2, pp. 88–9, 95, 101–2 (for 28 October and 30 October sessions) and no. 3, pp. 87–96 (for 31 October and 1 November sessions).

### DOCUMENT 23   GOMUŁKA ADDRESSING POLISH WRITERS, 5 JUNE 1963

*This is part of Gomułka's speech to the editorial boards of the literary journals* Nowa Kultura *and* Przegląd Kulturalny *explaining why he had decided to close them both down and set up a new journal,* Kultura, *which would be less unorthodox and not make criticisms of the party and the government.*

If you look around you at the other socialist countries of our camp, you will not come across any country so far behind in the building, in the construction, of socialist relations as Poland. Above all we have the big private economic sector of small-scale peasant production. This admittedly derives from the politics, the political line, of our party. We consider that a different approach would be inappropriate, and would not produce the results we require. But this does not alter the fact that with us peasant production is still an essential branch of our economy. This is small commodity production, in reality capitalist production. And the psychology and world-view of such a person is that produced by capitalist conditions. ... The second fact that distinguishes our country from others is this: the monopoly exerted by the Catholic Church in the area of religious belief. And religious believers are the overwhelming majority of our society. We know the position of the episcopate is hostile to socialism. This puts a significant curb on the scope of the formation of the nation's socialist consciousness. We ought to be much further along the road of building socialism, and particularly the transformation of social consciousness in a socialist spirit. But we are not. This is why we must be careful. ... It is not that we demand an absence of criticism, that we want to return to what happened in the past. But we demand a straightforward socialist attitude. What is important is not the literary form of expression but the political content.

> A. Garlicki, *Z Tajnych Archiwów*, Polska Oficyna Wydawnicza 'BGW', Warsaw, 1993,
> pp. 280–1, 288.

## DOCUMENT 24  THE ACTION PROGRAMME OF THE COMMUNIST PARTY OF CZECHOSLOVAKIA, 5 APRIL 1968

*This document expresses the ideas of the communist reformers during the 'Prague Spring' of 1968 in Czechoslovakia. The original is very long, and here we shall simply quote the most important passages.*

### Developing Democracy and Eliminating Equalitarianism

The Party has often criticised equalitarian views, but in practice levelling has spread to an unheard of extent and become one of the impediments to an intensive development of the economy and raising the living standard.

### The Leading Role of the Party – A Guarantee of Socialist Progress

The Communist Party enjoys the voluntary support of the people. It does not practice its leading role by ruling society but by most devotedly serving its free, progressive socialist development. The Party cannot enforce its authority. Authority must be won again and again by Party activity. The Party's goal is not to become a universal 'caretaker' of the society but to arouse socialist initiative and win over all the workers to communism through systematic persuasion and personal example.

### No Responsibility Without Rights

The National Front ... does not create opposition to state policy or lead struggles for political power. The leading political principle in the National Front is the Marxist-Leninist concept. The CPCz will ensure its leading role in a democratic way. The National Front must be granted independent rights and responsibility for the management of our country and society.

Legal norms must provide a more precise guarantee of *freedom of speech for minority interests and opinions*. The constitutional freedom of *movement*, particularly that of travel abroad, *must be precisely guaranteed by law.*

## The Equality of Czechs and Slovaks is the Basis for the Strength of the Republic

There are serious faults in the constitutional arrangement of relations between Czechs and Slovaks. It is necessary to effect a crucial change in this, and to draw up and pass a constitutional law to embody the principle of a symmetrical arrangement as the goal to work towards. This law will settle the status of Slovak national bodies in our constitutional system on the basis of full equality.

## The National Economy and the Standard of Living

The system of protectionism – furthering economic backwardness, and maintained by our policy of prices, subsidies and grants – continues to prevail in our economic policy. This creates conditions under which ineffective, poorly managed enterprises may not only exist but are often given preference. It is not possible to blunt economic policy for ever by taking from those who work well and giving to those who work badly. Differences in income between enterprises should reflect actual differences in the level of their economic activities.

R.A. Remington, [18], pp. 97, 98, 103, 105, 107, 114, 115, 120, 133.

---

DOCUMENT 25    **TWO CRITICAL VIEWS OF THE PRAGUE SPRING**

*Two statements by opponents of communism are included here. Czecho-slovakia in 1968 was the only place and time at which such views could be openly published. This was one reason for the Soviet decision of August 1968 to suppress the Czechoslovak experiment. Václav Havel, already well known in 1968 as a satirical playwright, was one of the most active dissi-dents of the 1970s and 1980s, later becoming President of Czechoslovakia. Ivan Sviták was a philosophy professor and perhaps the most radical oppo-sition voice to be heard in 1968.*

1   Václav Havel:

To begin with, why is it that the ideas put forward so far seem to sound so half-hearted? We hear quite often that the natural function of opposition will be carried out quite simply by public opinion, kept well informed by the mass media. The trouble is that democracy is not a matter of *faith*, but of guarantees. ... I think it an illusion that the internal democratization of the party would provide a sufficient guarantee of democracy...

The most logical and acceptable solution would be the constitution of an opposition by the revival of the existing non-communist parties in the National Front. But I myself do not have much faith in this solution. Over the past twenty years these parties ... have compromised themselves too much. ... Let's be honest about this. You can only talk about democracy seriously when people occasionally have the opportunity of freely electing who is to govern them. This assumes that *two comparable alternatives* exist, each of which has an equal chance of becoming the leading force in society. The only effective way of reaching the ideal of democratic socialism is a *two party model* based on a socialist social organization. ... The two parties would be able to relate to each other in a new kind of *coalition*. They could be linked by an agreement about their common aim: the self-realization of the nation through democratic socialism. ...

In conclusion I would like to mention something which is very important. ... Just what am I asking for? Nothing other than the demand for the complete rehabilitation of all non-communists, who have had to suffer for their conviction that a socialism which was prepared to sacrifice democracy and liberty could not be good. ... The 80,000 political prisoners from the fifties have been through so hard a test of their moral strength and character that it would be an unpardonable sin if this force was not actively integrated into the nation's spiritual life.

There is something else: the problem of the post-February political and non-political exiles. All of these people are still regarded as enemies of the people and of the country. Many of them emigrated because they were threatened with imprisonment or persecution...

Unless the state's attitude to these exiles is revised, the situation here, among ourselves, cannot be fully normalized.

First published in *Literární listy*, 4 April 1968, and translated in A. Oxley, A. Pravda and A. Ritchie, *Czechoslovakia. The Party and the People*, Allen Lane, 1973, pp. 131, 132, 134, 135, 137, 139 and 140.

2   Ivan Sviták: 'With Your Head Against the Wall' (extracts from a lecture given on 20 March 1968)

If we look in a matter-of-fact and critical manner at the results of the three months of the process of regeneration, we must note that, with the sole exception of the temporary absence of censorship, no structural changes have taken place in the mechanism of totalitarian dictatorship. The monopoly of a single party over political life continues unchanged, and in the meantime there exist none of the procedures customarily used in a democracy to create the political will of the people. There is only one element at present which justifies us in being optimistic about the democratization process, and that is the way public opinion is genuinely being expressed. It is therefore exactly there that the counterattack of the forces of conservatism will be directed very soon indeed. They will call for moderation and suggest new economic reforms and persons in place of fundamental political changes. Our endeavour, in contrast, must be fully to utilize the tolerated limits of freedom in order to enforce democratic elections as a further element in the move towards a European socialist state.

The liquidation of the mechanisms of totalitarian dictatorship and totalitarian thought is a prerequisite to the attainment of democratic socialism. If the question is posed 'Whence, whither and with whom' one can reply briefly: 'From Asia to Europe, by ourselves.' The meaning of this is: from totalitarian dictatorship to an open society, to the liquidation of the power monopoly and to effective control of the power élite by means of a free press and public opinion. The intellectuals of this country must lay claim to leading an open socialist society towards democracy and humanism if we are to avoid any continuation of the irrational dialectic of despotism and tyranny.

First published in *Student* (Prague), no. 15, on 10 April 1968. Reprinted in I. Sviták, *Kulatý Čtverec. Dialektika Demokratizace*, Naše Vojsko, Prague, 1990, pp. 31–2.

### DOCUMENT 26   THE CZECHOSLOVAK LEADERS AGONIZE ABOUT ANTI-SOCIALIST TENDENCIES, MAY 1968

*The Presidium of the Czechoslovak Communist Party met in May 1968 in a context of attacks from without and within. Dubček was severely criticized in Moscow early in May for failing to restrain anti-socialist forces. This extract shows that he was under pressure, not just from the conservatives, but from members of his own moderate reforming faction such as Smrkovský and Černík. It also demonstrates his continuing opposition to negative measures which would restrict the spontaneous support he sought from the population.*

Smrkovský: I still support the direction in which we have set out. Even so, things are moving a bit differently from the way we wanted them to. ... It is a fact that the people once again have hope when they look to the new policy of the party. But while we are making speeches and want to democratize our life, certain others are not rallying around the Action Programme but instead are preparing to launch a frontal attack on our position. ... What I am going to say is not something I have brought back from the Soviet Union. I want to point out that various forces are now rallying for a frontal attack on the position of the party. The mass media are from morning to night ferreting out all the bad things that have happened. I as a communist official certainly do not want to live to see a counter-revolution in this country. ...

Černík: The assault on the state apparatus is crystal clear. Even this workers' regime must rely on a strong state apparatus. It is interesting to note where the attack is being launched. It is not being launched against the ministries in charge of the economy, even though the economy is a weak spot. The attacks are being systematically directed against the army, the organs of state security, the police, the courts, the prosecutor's office and last but not least the party apparatus. I don't want to panic, but personally I am convinced that counter-revolution is on the advance in this country. ...

Dubček: As regards our next procedure, I think that what is essential are the socialist tendencies that, if not universal, are prevalent among the overwhelming majority. That is the decisive force. On the other hand, there are various pressure groups and efforts to form a political opposition. The first priority is to pursue what is positive, the socialist factor that endorses the policy of the party's CC.

Minutes of the Meeting of the Presidium of the CC of the CPCz held on 7–8 May 1968.

> J. Navrátil (ed.), *The Prague Spring '68. A National Security Archive Documents Reader*,
> Central European University Press, Budapest, 1998, Document 30, pp. 129–31.

### DOCUMENT 27    THE LETTER OF INVITATION FROM CZECHOSLOVAK HARD-LINERS TO L.I. BREZHNEV, AUGUST 1968

*This is the letter sent to Soviet leader L.I. Brezhnev inviting him to intervene in Czechoslovakia, which he read out at a Warsaw Pact meeting on 18 August 1968. The people who sent it always strenuously denied its existence but the original was handed to President Havel of Czechoslovakia in 1992 by his Russian counterpart Boris Yeltsin.*

Respected Leonid Ilyich!

We are turning to you with the following declaration in awareness of our full responsibility for the decision to do so.

Our post-January democratic process, which is essentially healthy, involving as it does the rectification of the errors and deficiencies of the past, and of the general political direction of society, has gradually been wrested from the hands of the Central Committee of our party. The press, radio and TV, which in practice find themselves in the hands of right-wing forces, have had such an influence on public opinion that now elements hostile to the party are beginning to take part in political life without meeting any resistance from the public. They are setting off a wave of nationalism and chauvinism, and calling forth an anti-communist and anti-Soviet psychosis.

The leadership of the party has committed a series of errors ... [It] is already incapable of successfully defending itself against attacks on socialism, incapable of organizing either ideological or political resistance to right-wing forces. The very essence of socialism in our country is under threat. Political agencies and agencies of state power in our country have at the present already become paralysed. Rightist forces have created favourable conditions for a counter-revolutionary coup. In such a grave situation we turn to you, a Soviet communist, and the leading representative of the CPSU and the Soviet Union, with the request that you give us genuine support and aid with all the means at your disposal. Only with your help can Czechoslovakia be extricated from the threatening danger of counter-revolution.

We are conscious that for the CPSU and the Soviet Union this final step for the defence of socialism in the Czechoslovak Socialist Republic would not be easy. We shall therefore fight with our own means and with all our strength. But if our forces and possibilities should turn out to be exhausted or if they do not bring positive results, then please consider this declaration to be a genuine appeal for all-round assistance. In view of the complexity and the dangers of the developing situation in our country, we ask you to observe maximum secrecy. For this reason we have written personally and directly to you in the Russian language.

Signed by: Alois Indra, Drahomír Kolder, Antonín Kapek, Oldřich Švestka and Vasil Bil'ak.

F. Janáček and M. Michálková, 'Příběh zvacího dopisu', *Soudobé Dějiny*, I, 1 (1993), pp. 94, 95.

## DOCUMENT 28   COMMUNIST PARTY MEMBERSHIP, 1939–50

| Country | 1939/41 | mid-1945 | 1947 | 1950 |
|---|---|---|---|---|
| Albania | – | – | 45,000 | |
| Bulgaria | 8,000 | 250,000 | 495,000 | 460,000 |
| Czechoslovakia | 60,000 | 500,000 | 1,300,000 | 2,300,000 |
| Hungary | 500 | 227,000 | 660,000 | 829,000 |
| Poland | 8,000 | 189,000 | 849,000 | 1,360,000 |
| Romania | 500 | 101,810 | 710,000 | 720,000 |
| Yugosavia | 12,000 | | 141,000 | 530,812 |

[57], *pp. 9–10, 236;* [104], *p. 81;* [156], *p. 181;* [168], *p. 305;* [177], *p. 65;* [180], *p. 149.*

(Birth rates per 1,000 people (increases in italics))

| Country | 1947 | 1954 | 1959 | 1966 | 1970 |
|---|---|---|---|---|---|
| Albania | | 40.9 | 43.4 | 34.0 | 35.3 |
| Bulgaria | 24.0 | 20.2 | 17.6 | 14.9 | 16.3 |
| Czechoslovakia | 24.2 | 20.6 | 16.0 | 15.6 | 15.8 |
| East Germany | | 16.8 | 17.2 | 15.8 | 13.9 |
| Hungary | 20.6 | 23.0 | 15.2 | 13.6 | 14.7 |
| Poland | 29.3 | 29.1 | 24.9 | 16.7 | 16.8 |
| Romania | 22.4 | 24.8 | 20.2 | 14.3 | 21.1 |
| Yugoslavia | 28.1 | 28.5 | 23.1 | 20.2 | 17.8 |

*United Nations Demographic Yearbook, 1955*, United Nations, New York, 1955, p. 617; *United Nations Demographic Yearbook, 1960*, United Nations, New York, 1960, pp. 485–7; *United Nations Demographic Yearbook, 1971*, United Nations, New York, 1972, pp. 637–9.

| | 1948 | 1968 | fall, 1948–68 |
|---|---|---|---|
| **South Eastern Europe** | | | |
| Albania | 121.2 | 86.8 | 28.3% |
| Bulgaria | 118.2 | 28.3 | 76.1% |
| Romania | 142.7 | 59.5 | 58.3% |
| Yugoslavia | 102.1 | 58.6 | 42.9% |
| Greece | 41.9 | 34.4 | 17.9% |
| **East Central Europe** | | | |
| Czechoslovakia | 83.5 | 22.1 | 73.5% |
| East Germany | 89.1 | 20.4 | 77.1% |
| Hungary | 94.1 | 35.8 | 62.0% |
| Poland | 111.1 | 33.4 | 69.9% |
| West Germany | 68.1 | 22.8 | 66.5% |

*United Nations Demographic Yearbook, 1956*, United Nations, New York, 1956, pp. 691–2; *United Nations Demographic Yearbook, 1971*, United Nations, New York, 1971, pp. 669–71.

## DOCUMENT 31   LIFE EXPECTANCY AT AGE 1 (YEARS OF LIFE)

|  | early 1930s | | late 1940s | | mid-1960s | | increase (in years) | |
| --- | --- | --- | --- | --- | --- | --- | --- | --- |
|  | M | F | M | F | M | F | M | F |
| **South East Europe** | | | | | | | | |
| Albania |  |  |  |  | 69.6 | 72.2 |  |  |
| Bulgaria | 54.4 | 53.7 |  |  | 70.3 | 73.8 | 15.9 | 20.1 |
| Romania |  |  |  |  | 69.4 | 73.0 |  |  |
| Yugoslavia | 57.8 | 60.6 | 63.5 | 65.3 | 67.3 | 70.3 | 9.5 | 9.7 |
| Greece | 53.2 | 55.1 |  |  | 70.5 | 73.5 | 17.3 | 18.4 |
| **East Central Europe** | | | | | | | | |
| Czechoslovakia | 59.9 | 62.0 |  |  | 68.2 | 74.1 | 8.3 | 12.1 |
| East Germany |  |  | 68.2 | 71.4 | 69.5 | 74.2 | 1.3 | 2.8 |
| Hungary |  |  | 64.5 | 68.0 | 69.1 | 73.5 | 4.6 | 5.5 |
| Poland |  |  | 62.5 | 67.4 | 69.0 | 74.4 | 6.5 | 7.0 |
| West Germany |  |  | 67.8 | 71.0 | 68.4 | 74.1 | 0.6 | 2.9 |

*United Nations Demographic Yearbook, 1951*, United Nations, New York, 1951, pp. 532–6;
*United Nations Demographic Yearbook, 1952*, United Nations, New York, 1952, pp. 448–50;
*United Nations Demographic Yearbook, 1971*, United Nations, 1972, pp. 760–2.

## DOCUMENT 32   HOUSING FACILITIES

| Country | Persons per room | | Piped water (%) | | Electricity (%) | |
| --- | --- | --- | --- | --- | --- | --- |
|  | 1950 | 1965–70 | 1950 | 1965–70 | 1950 | 1965–70 |
| Bulgaria | 2.0 | 1.2 | 7.0 | 28.5 |  | 94.8 |
| Czechoslovakia | 1.6 | 1.3 | 35.6 | 49.1 | 85.2 | 97.3 |
| Hungary | 1.6 | 1.2 | 23.0 | 36.4 | 63.0 | 92.1 |
| Poland | 1.8 | 1.7 |  | 46.8 |  | 80.1 |
| Romania |  | 1.4 |  | 12.3 |  | 48.6 |
| Yugoslavia | 2.4 | 1.6 | 26.9 | 42.4 |  | 54.5 |

After: M.C. Kaser and E.A. Radice (eds), [79], *p. 343*; C. Gati (ed.), [72], *p. 373*.

## DOCUMENT 33    GROSS DOMESTIC PRODUCT PER CAPITA (INDEX = 100)

|  |  | *1948* | *1965* |
|---|---|---|---|
| United Kingdom |  | 100 | 100 |
| Bulgaria |  | 16 | 45 |
| Czechoslovakia |  | 49 | 74 |
| German Democratic Republic |  | 43 | 74 |
| Hungary |  | 24 | 53 |
| Poland |  | 35 | 51 |
| Romania |  | 19 | 36 |
| Yugoslavia | (1937) | 18 | 36 |

Author's calculations, based on figures of dollar GDP per capita at constant 1963 values given in *Economic Survey of Europe in 1969, Part I* [71], p. 9.

# CHRONOLOGY

## 1944

| | |
|---|---|
| 22 July | Polish Committee of National Liberation (PKWN) set up by Stalin as a provisional government for liberated areas of Poland. |
| 23 August | King Michael of Romania changes sides, abandoning the Axis powers. |
| 8 September | Bulgaria declares war on Germany. |
| September | Tito meets Stalin in Moscow and urges him to order Soviet army units to enter Yugoslavia immediately; Stalin does this. |
| October | Churchill and Stalin make the 'percentage agreement' dividing Eastern Europe. National Democratic Front set up in Romania. |
| 21 December | Hungarian Provisional Government set up in Debrecen. |

## 1945

| | |
|---|---|
| 1 January | The PKWN becomes the Provisional Government of Poland. |
| 4–11 February | Conference at Yalta (Crimea) between British Prime Minister Churchill, US President Roosevelt and Soviet leader Stalin. |
| 27 February | Soviet envoy Vyshinsky forces King Michael of Romania to appoint Petru Groza as Prime Minister. |
| 8 May | End of the Second World War in Europe. |
| 9 June | Soviet Military Administration in Germany (SMAD) is set up. |
| 17 July–2 August | Potsdam Conference of the victorious Allies. |
| 4 November | Elections in Hungary: Smallholders gain 57 per cent; HCP 17 per cent. |
| November | Soviet occupation forces withdraw from Czechoslovakia. |
| 16–26 December | Moscow Conference held. It recommends inclusion of non-communists in Bulgarian and Romanian governments and free elections. |

## 1946

| | |
|---|---|
| 21–22 April | Social Democratic–Communist merger sets up Socialist Unity Party (SED) in East Germany. |
| 26 May | Elections in Czechoslovakia: the CPCz receives 38 per cent of the vote. |

**1947**

| | |
|---|---|
| 19 January | Parliamentary elections in Poland. The communist-run Democratic Bloc wins 80.1 per cent of the vote. |
| 10 February | Peace treaties signed with Bulgaria, Hungary and Romania. |
| 26 February | Arrest of Béla Kovács, leader of the Smallholders' Party (Hungary). |
| 10 July | Czechoslovak government decides not to take part in the Marshall Plan. |
| 16 August | Trial of Nikola Petkov (Bulgarian Agrarian leader) ends. He is sentenced to death by hanging. |
| 31 August | Elections in Hungary. Government coalition secures 60.9 per cent of the vote. |
| 22–27 September | A conference in Poland sets up the Communist Information Bureau (Cominform). |
| October | Trial of Dragoljub Jovanović (Yugoslav Agrarian leader); he is sentenced to nine years' imprisonment. |

**1948**

| | |
|---|---|
| 25 February | The 'Prague coup'. The communists exclude their partners from power in Czechoslovakia. |
| 28 June | The Cominform meets and passes a resolution against the Yugoslav leader Tito and his associates. |
| 3 September | Gomułka is condemned and replaced as Polish party leader by Bierut. |
| 15–21 December | Unification Congress of Polish socialist and communist parties sets up the Polish United Workers' Party (PZPR). |

**1949**

| | |
|---|---|
| 11 June | Albanian Minister of the Interior Koçi Xoxe is executed for treason. |
| 22 September | Show trial of László Rajk, former Hungarian Minister of the Interior, ends with the death sentence. |
| 7 October | The German Democratic Republic (GDR) is established. |
| 15 October | Rajk is hanged. |
| 16 December | Traicho Kostov, former Bulgarian communist leader, is hanged. |

**1950**

| | |
|---|---|
| 27 June | Basic Law on Workers' Self-Management issued in Yugoslavia. |

**1952**

| | |
|---|---|
| 10 March | Stalin sends a note to the Western powers offering to reunify Germany. |
| 12 July | Second Party Conference of the SED proclaims 'building of socialism' in the GDR as its aim. |
| 20–27 November | Show trial of Rudolf Slánský and thirteen other Czechoslovak communists. |
| November | The Yugoslav Communist Party, at its Fifth Congress, is renamed the League of Communists of Yugoslavia (LCY). |

**1953**

| | |
|---|---|
| 5 March | Death of Stalin. |
| 14–16 June | The Hungarian communist leaders are severely criticized in Moscow by the post–Stalin leadership and Imre Nagy is appointed Prime Minister with a mandate to implement the 'New Course'. |
| 17 June | Strikes and demonstrations in the GDR against higher work norms; suppressed by Soviet troops. |

**1954**

| | |
|---|---|
| 17 January | Milovan Djilas is expelled from the Central Committee of the LCY for suggesting the withering away of the League. |

**1955**

| | |
|---|---|
| 18 April | Imre Nagy is replaced as Prime Minister of Hungary by András Hegedűs. |
| 26 May–2 June | Soviet leaders visit Belgrade and restore state relations with Yugoslavia. |

**1956**

| | |
|---|---|
| 14–25 February | Twentieth Party Congress of the CPSU. Khrushchev denounces Stalin in a secret speech. |
| 17 April | Dissolution of the Cominform. |
| 28–29 June | Riots in Poznań (Poland) put down with severe loss of life. |
| 21 July | Rákosi replaced by Gerő at the head of the Hungarian Workers' Party. |
| 20 October | Eighth Plenum of the PZPR. Gomułka is restored to the Polish leadership. |
| 23 October | Mass demonstrations in Budapest begin the Hungarian revolution. |
| 24 October | First Soviet military intervention in Hungary. |

| | |
|---|---|
| 27 October | Formation in Hungary of the People's Patriotic Government under Imre Nagy. |
| 4 November | Second Soviet military intervention in Hungary; János Kádár sets up a Hungarian Revolutionary Worker–Peasant Government on Soviet territory. |

*1957*

| | |
|---|---|
| 20 January | Relatively free elections to the Polish parliament. Non-party candidates gain 13.8 per cent of the seats. |

*1958*

| | |
|---|---|
| May | Withdrawal of Soviet troops from Romania. |
| 16 June | Execution of Imre Nagy after a secret trial. |

*1961*

| | |
|---|---|
| 13 August | Construction starts on the Berlin Wall, dividing East and West Berlin |
| 17–31 October | Twenty-Second Congress of the CPSU. Khrushchev again denounces Stalin. |

*1962*

| | |
|---|---|
| 20–24 November | Eighth Congress of the HSWP. Kádár announces a 'one nation' policy. |

*1963*

| | |
|---|---|
| March | Final amnesty in Hungary releases remaining prisoners from 1956. |
| April | The Kolder Commission recommends rehabilitation of some purge victims. |

*1964*

| | |
|---|---|
| 13 October | Khrushchev is removed from power in the Soviet Union and is replaced by Brezhnev. |

*1965*

| | |
|---|---|
| 19 March | Nicolae Ceauşescu becomes Romanian party leader. |

*1966*

| | |
|---|---|
| March | The Albanian 'cultural revolution' starts with a campaign against bureaucracy. |
| July | Ranković is dismissed as head of Yugoslav state security. |

### 1967

| | |
|---|---|
| June | Czechoslovak writers criticize many aspects of party policy at their Fourth Congress. |
| September | Enver Hoxha announces victory in the struggle against religion in Albania. |

### 1968

| | |
|---|---|
| 1 January | New Economic Mechanism introduced in Hungary. |
| 3 January | Antonín Novotný is removed from the office of First Secretary of the CPCz; his replacement is Alexander Dubček. |
| 8 March | Student demonstrations in Poland; violently repressed, followed by a fierce campaign against Zionists and revisionists. |
| 21 March | Novotný resigns as President of Czechoslovakia and is succeeded by General Svoboda. |
| 10 April | The Action Programme of the CPCz is published. |
| June | Students demonstrate in Belgrade against party privileges and for political freedom. |
| 20 June | Warsaw Pact manoeuvres start on Czechoslovak territory. |
| 25 June | Czechoslovak National Assembly votes to end censorship and rehabilitate victims of Stalinist repression. |
| 27 June | The 'Two Thousand Words' Manifesto is published, calling on the people of Czechoslovakia to take action to defeat forces hostile to the process of democratization. |
| 15 July | The Warsaw Letter complaining that the CPCz has lost control of events in Czechoslovakia is published. |
| 20–21 August | Czechoslovakia is invaded during the night by Warsaw Pact forces. |
| 22 August | The 'Fourteenth Congress' of the CPCz is held in secret in a Prague suburb: it votes to condemn Soviet intervention and removes all opponents of reform from the party leadership. |
| 27 August | The Moscow Agreement is signed between Czechoslovak and Soviet representatives. The Czechoslovaks agree to 'normalize' the situation, and the Dubček leadership is restored to office. |

### 1969

| | |
|---|---|
| 16 January | Suicide of Jan Palach in Prague in protest against the re-introduction of censorship. |
| 28 March | The Prague office of the Soviet airline Aeroflot is destroyed by Czech demonstrators. |
| 17 April | Dubček is replaced by Husák as First Secretary of the CPCz, and a new party Presidium is elected from which all reformers except Dubček are excluded. |
| September | Dubček is removed from the Presidium and the 'Fourteenth Congress' is declared illegal and its decisions null and void. |

# GLOSSARY

*ACCs (Allied Control Commissions)* Joint United States–Soviet–United Kingdom authorities set up in 1944 to administer certain occupied enemy countries, including Bulgaria, Romania and Hungary.

*AK (Home Army)* The non-communist Polish resistance army during the Second World War.

*ÁVH (State Defence Authority)* The new name for the Hungarian security service, adopted in December 1949.

*AVNOJ (Anti-Fascist Council of the People's Liberation of Yugoslavia)* The political wing of the Yugoslav communists' National Army of Liberation, set up in November 1942, which in effect became a provisional government of Yugoslavia in November 1943.

*ÁVO (State Defence Department)* The Hungarian security service, set up in 1945.

*CC (Central Committee)* The governing body of a communist party, elected at each Congress of the party, and in theory the supreme authority between Congresses.

*četnici* (sing. *četnik*) Serbian irregular forces which emerged after 1941. They owed allegiance to the exiled royal Yugoslav government in London.

*CMEA (Council for Mutual Economic Assistance)* The body set up in 1949 to co-ordinate the economies of the Soviet bloc countries.

*Comecon* The name normally used in the West for the CMEA.

*Cominform* The usual Western designation of the Information Bureau of the Communist Parties which was set up in 1947 and lasted until 1956.

*CPCz (Communist Party of Czechoslovakia)* Founded in 1921, this party, unlike most others, did not change its name in 1948 after absorbing the Social Democrats.

*CPSU (Communist Party of the Soviet Union)* The name adopted in 1952 by the ruling communist party in the Soviet Union, which previously bore the name AUCP(b), or All-Union Communist Party (bolsheviks).

*CPY (Communist Party of Yugoslavia)* Set up in 1920, this party took control of Yugoslavia in 1945. It was renamed the League of Communists of Yugoslavia in 1952.

*DGSP (General Directorate of Popular Security)* The Romanian security service which was established in 1948 under Gheorghe Pintilie, alongside three deputies from the Soviet secret police. It is commonly referred to as the Securitate.

*GDR (German Democratic Republic)* The official name of the state set up in the Soviet Occupation Zone of Germany in 1949.

*HCP (Hungarian Communist Party)* The communist party which existed in Hungary between 1919 and 1948.

*HSWP (Hungarian Socialist Workers' Party)*   The name adopted by the re-founded HWP in November 1956.

*HWP (Hungarian Workers' Party)*   The name adopted by the HCP after the merger with the Social Democrats in 1948.

*JZD (Unified Agricultural Cooperative)*   The Czechoslovak version of a collective farm.

*KBW (Corps for Internal Security)*   The Polish internal security force set up in May 1945. It was subordinated in 1946, along with the UB, to the State Security Committee.

*KGB (Committee for State Security)*   The title of the Soviet state security apparatus from 1954 onwards.

*kolkhozy*   The Russian expression for collective farms. Communist governments in Eastern Europe avoided using this term, preferring to describe their collective farms as cooperatives.

*KPD (Communist Party of Germany)*   Founded in 1919, this party existed underground after 1933 and re-emerged after Nazi Germany was defeated in 1945.

*KRN (National Council of the Homeland)*   The underground committee set up in Poland in December 1943 by the communists along with a few left-wing allies.

*KSRs (Conferences of Workers' Self-Management)*   The organizations set up in Poland in 1958 to incorporate the Workers' Councils alongside various management and trade union bodies.

*LCY (League of Communists of Yugoslavia)*   The name adopted in 1952 by the communist party, and retained until 1990.

*LPGs (Agricultural Production Cooperatives)*   The name used for the collective farms introduced from 1952 onwards in East Germany.

*Marshall Plan*   The plan for European economic recovery put forward by the United States in June 1947 and accepted by Western but not Eastern European governments.

*MEFESZ (Federation of Hungarian University and College Students' Associations)*   The Hungarian student association which was set up independently of the official communist youth organization in 1956.

*MGB (Ministry of State Security)*   The ministry formed in 1946 to run the Soviet state security organs.

*NKVD (People's Commissariat for Internal Affairs)*   The title used for the Soviet political police between 1934 and 1946.

*OZNA (Bureau for the People's Protection)*   The title of the Yugoslav communist secret police until 1946, when it was renamed UDBA.

*PKWN (Polish Committee of National Liberation)*   The body set up on 20 July 1944 to administer the parts of Poland freed from Nazi occupation by the Red Army. It was also known as the 'Lublin government', to distinguish it from its rival, the 'London government in exile'.

*PPR (Polish Workers' Party)*   The name taken by the Polish communist party when it was re-founded in January 1942.

*PPS (Polish Socialist Party)* The traditional party of Polish socialists which split, during the Second World War, into two groups, the leftist RPPS and the WRN. The PPS was re-founded in September 1944, with the support of members of both groups, although part of the WRN continued to exist separately until it was suppressed by the new Polish government. The main body of the PPS merged with the PPR in December 1948 to form the PZPR.

*Presidium* This replaced the Politbureau as the supreme governing body of the CPSU in 1952. The name was changed back to Politbureau in 1966.

*PSL (Polish Peasant Party)* The name of the party set up in 1945, comprising members of the prewar SL who did not favour an alliance with the communists. Between 1945 and 1947 the PSL fought under its leader Mikołajczyk against the communist seizure of power. After 1947 the party was taken over by pro-communists, and in 1949 it was merged with the pro-communist SL to form the ZSL.

*PZPR (Polish United Workers' Party)* The name taken by the PPR after it absorbed the PPS in December 1948.

*ROH (Revolutionary Trade Union Movement)* The unified trade union movement in Czechoslovakia which was under communist control from 1945 onwards.

*SBZ (Soviet Occupation Zone)* The official title from 1945 to 1949 of the area of Germany which was under Soviet occupation.

*SED (Socialist Unity Party of Germany)* The name taken by the communist party in East Germany after its absorption of the East German Social Democrats in 1946.

*SL (Peasant Party)* This refers to the pro-communist party which emerged out of one faction of the prewar peasant party (also SL) in Poland after 1945. In 1949 it absorbed the surviving rump of the PSL and, under the name ZSL, became the communists' agrarian partner.

*SPD (Social Democratic Party of Germany)* This party, which had enjoyed a continuous existence since 1890, re-emerged after the defeat of the Nazis in both West and East Germany, but only survived in the West.

*Staatssicherheitsdienst (State Security Service)* The security service set up in the GDR after 1949.

*StB (State Security)* The Czechoslovak state security force.

*TOZ (Association for the Joint Cultivation of the Land)* The loosest form of agricultural cooperative, favoured in the Soviet Union during the mid-1920s.

*UB (Security Office)* The Polish secret police, subordinated after 1946 to the State Security Committee.

*UDBA (Administration of State Security)* The Yugoslav secret police force after 1946.

*ustaše (sing. ustaša) (rebels)* The *ustaše* started as an extreme nationalist grouping in Croatia in the 1930s. In 1941 they were given effective control of the Croat puppet state set up by the Nazis on former Yugoslav territory; they became notorious for their massacres of Jews and Serbs.

*USSR (Union of Soviet Socialist Republics)* The official title of the Soviet Union.

*Warsaw Pact*   The military alliance set up in 1955 between the Soviet Union and all the Eastern European countries except Yugoslavia.

*Wiesław*   The party pseudonym of the Polish communist leader Władysław Gomułka.

*WRN* (*Freedom, Equality, Independence*)   The pro-London, anti-communist majority faction of the PPS. After 1944 some of its members went over to the refounded PPS, while others remained outside.

*ZSL* (*United Peasant Party*)   The Polish peasant party formed in 1949 by the merger between the PSL and the SL.

*Zveno* (*The Link*)   The Bulgarian periodical which gave its name to a group of politicians who favoured the modernization of the country by authoritarian means and briefly exercised power in coalition with the communists after 1944.

# WHO'S WHO

*Beneš, Edward (1884–1948)*  President of Czechoslovakia from 1935 to 1938 and again from 1940, in exile, and from 1945 to 1948, at home again. Staked his political future on cooperation with the Soviet Union in 1943. Resigned in June 1948, having failed to prevent the communist seizure of power in February.

*Beria, Lavrenti Pavlovich (1899–1953)*  Soviet secret policeman, and head of the NKVD from 1938 onwards. Soviet Minister of the Interior from 1942 to 1946. Took part in moves towards a 'New Course' after Stalin's death. Removed from office and arrested in July 1953 and shot shortly afterwards.

*Berman, Jakub (1901–84)*  Polish communist leader. Joined the party in the 1920s. In exile in the Soviet Union after 1939. Helped to found the Central Bureau of Polish Communists in the USSR in 1943. Various government posts after 1945. Remained in the Politbureau until May 1956. Regarded as jointly responsible for the Stalinist measures of the early 1950s. Expelled from the party in 1957 for this.

*Bibó, István (1911–74)*  Hungarian social thinker, active after 1945 in the National Peasant Party. Served in the Imre Nagy government during the 1956 revolution. Imprisoned, 1957–63. Theorist of Hungarian populism and advocate of a multi-party socialist system.

*Bierut, Bolesław (1892–1956)*  Polish communist leader. Underground activity up to arrest in 1935. President of the KRN, 1944–47. President of the Polish Republic, 1947–52. Head of the PPR, September 1948–December 1948. Head of the PZPR, December 1948–March 1956 and thus in effect ruler of the country.

*Brezhnev, Leonid Il'ich (1906–82)*  General Secretary of the CPSU from 1964 to 1982. Ordered the invasion of Czechoslovakia in 1968. His period of office in the Soviet Union is usually regarded as an era of immobility and stagnation.

*Byrnes, James Francis (1879–1972)*  United States Secretary of State from 1945 to 1947. A close associate of President Roosevelt after whose death in 1945 Byrnes tried to preserve the good wartime relationship between the USA and the Soviet Union. Increasing differences of view with the new president, Harry Truman, led to Byrnes's resignation from office in January 1947.

*Ceauşescu, Nicolae (1918–89)*  Romanian communist. Joined the party in 1933 at the age of fifteen. In prison from 1936 to 1944. Held various party and government posts from 1944 to 1965. Succeeded Gheorghiu-Dej as General Secretary of the party in 1965. Prime Minister from 1967. Ruled the country dictatorially until 1989 when he was overthrown in the revolution and killed.

*Clementis, Vladimír (1902–52)*  Slovak communist. Deputy Minister of Foreign Affairs from 1945 to 1948. Foreign Minister from 1948 to 1950. Purged, tried on charges of Titoism and bourgeois nationalism, and hanged in 1952.

*Dimitrov, Georgi Mikhailovich (1882–1949)* Veteran Bulgarian communist, mainly active in the Communist International from its foundation until its dissolution in 1943. Spent the Second World War in the Soviet Union. Returned to Bulgaria in November 1945 to take charge of the communist party. Prime Minister from 1946 to 1949.

*Djilas, Milovan (1911–95)* Yugoslav communist and political writer. Born in Montenegro, a partisan leader during the Second World War. Politbureau member from 1940 to 1954. Expelled from the party for his writings on the emergence of a new class of communist party bureaucrats. Imprisoned from 1956 to 1961. Re-arrested in 1962 for his book *Conversations with Stalin*. Released in 1966. Rehabilitated in 1989.

*Dubček, Alexander (1921–92)* Slovak communist who rose to be leader of the Slovak Communist Party from 1963 and a member of the Czechoslovak Party Presidium from 1964. In January 1968 he was elected First Secretary of the CPCz. He presided over the experiment in 'socialism with a human face' which was ended by the Soviet invasion of August 1968. After his removal from office in April 1969 Dubček was demoted to become, successively, Ambassador to Turkey and an employee of the Slovak forestry department. He returned to politics in 1989 but never regained his former popularity.

*Gerő, Ernő (1898–1980)* Second most important Hungarian communist leader after 1945. Spent the 1920s and 1930s, and the Second World War, in the Soviet Union. Returned home in 1945. Briefly replaced Rákosi as head of the party in 1956. In semi-exile in the Soviet Union from 1956 to 1960.

*Gheorghiu-Dej, Gheorghe (1901–65)* Member of the Romanian Communist Party from 1930. After spending the war in prison he became party leader in 1944, attaining sole power by purging his rivals Ana Pauker and Vasile Luca in 1952. In the 1960s he adopted a 'national communist' policy of preserving neutrality in the Sino-Soviet dispute and resisting Soviet efforts to achieve greater economic integration through the CMEA.

*Gomułka, Władysław (1905–82)* Polish communist. Joined the party in the 1920s, spent long periods in prison in Poland, escaped, and became the head of the newly founded PPR in November 1943. Held various government posts after 1944. Purged in August 1948 for right-wing deviation. Expelled from the PZPR in 1949. Arrested in 1951. Released in 1954. Headed the PZPR, and in effect the country, from October 1956 to December 1970.

*Gottwald, Klement (1896–1953)* Czech communist. Elected General Secretary of the CPCz in 1929. Became Prime Minister of Czechoslovakia in 1946. Exchanged this office for the Presidency of Czechoslovakia in 1948. Remained President until his death. He was an orthodox communist and follower of Stalin, who carried out whatever instructions came from Moscow, although he hesitated in 1948 over the collectivization of agriculture.

*Havel, Václav (1936– )* Leading Czech playwright. A prominent advocate of radical reform in 1968, including the return to a multi-party democratic system. His work was banned in Czechoslovakia after 1969. Subsequently, he led the dissident movement and eventually became President of Czechoslovakia in December 1989.

*Hoxha, Enver (1908–85)*   Leader of Albanian communism from 1941 onwards. After the victory of the communist partisans in 1945 he held the offices of Prime Minister and Foreign Minister until 1953. From 1954 until his death he was Secretary General of the Albanian Party of Labour (the communist party) and in effect the ruler of his country.

*Husák, Gustáv (1913–91)*   Slovak communist. Member of the CPCz from 1934. Headed the Communist Party of Slovakia from December 1944 to April 1945. Held various party posts until his arrest in 1951. In prison until 1960. Took charge of the country after the removal of the Dubček leadership in April 1969. Remained First Secretary of the CPCz until December 1987.

*Kádár, János (1912–89)*   Hungarian communist. Joined the party in 1931. In prison during the 1930s. Headed the communist party in Budapest between 1945 and 1948. Minister of the Interior from 1948 to 1950. Dismissed in 1950 and expelled from the party. In prison between 1951 and 1954. Restored to the party's Politbureau in July 1956. Re-founded the party in November 1956 as Hungarian Socialist Workers' Party and ran Hungary after the Soviet invasion as both Prime Minister and party leader. Oversaw a period of harsh repression but also moved to more moderate policies after 1961. Removed from power in 1988.

*Kardelj, Edvard (1910–79)*   Yugoslav communist of Slovene origin. Joined the party in 1928. Entered the Central Committee in 1937. A close colleague of Tito in the partisan movement and afterwards. Foreign Minister from 1948 to 1953. A leading ideologist of the party, he developed many of the distinctive policies of the post-1950 era.

*Khrushchev, Nikita Sergeevich (1894–1971)*   Soviet leader. First Secretary of the CPSU from 1953 to 1964, and Soviet Prime Minister from 1958 to 1964. Launched efforts at de-Stalinization both in 1956 and 1961, but also showed his determination to retain control of Eastern Europe by deciding to intervene in Hungary in 1956.

*Kołakowski, Leszek (1927– )*   Polish philosopher. Active in the intellectual movement to revise Marxism during the mid-1950s. Tolerated initially by the party leadership but expelled from the party for 'revisionism' in 1966. Dismissed from his professorship in 1968 and driven into exile.

*Kuroń, Jacek (1934– )*   Polish dissident intellectual. Expelled from the party twice, in 1953 and 1956. Imprisoned from 1965 to 1968 for issuing an 'Open Letter to the Party' which called for a workers' revolution to overthrow the existing bureaucracy and establish a system of Workers' Councils. Prominent in the student protest movement of 1968. Later a founder member of the Solidarity movement. Active in politics after 1989.

*Lukács, George (1885–1971)*   Hungarian philosopher and Marxist literary theorist. Founder member of the HCP, member of the Hungarian Soviet government of 1919. Subsequently in exile in Vienna and Moscow until his return in 1945. Minister of Popular Culture in the government of Imre Nagy during the 1956 revolution. Interned briefly in Romania. Restored to favour in 1963.

*Malenkov, Georgi Maksimilianovich (1902–88)*   Soviet leader, close to the top during the Second World War. Succeeded Stalin as Prime Minister in 1953. Associated with the 'New Course' adopted after Stalin's death. Removed from office in 1955. Expelled from the party in 1961 and sent to run a power station in Kazakhstan.

*Mihailović, Dragoljub (1893–1946)*   Yugoslav soldier, leader of the *četnik* guerrilla movement during the Second World War, which owed allegiance to the royal Yugoslav government-in-exile in London. Lost the support of the Allies in 1943 because of his dealings with the Axis. Tried and shot for treason after the communist victory in Yugoslavia.

*Mikołajczyk, Stanisław (1901–66)*   Founder of the Polish Peasant Party (PSL). Prime Minister of the Polish government-in-exile in London during the Second World War. Returned to Poland and joined the communist-dominated Provisional Government of National Unity in June 1945. Tried to retain some influence in the country over the next two years but fled in fear of his life in October 1947.

*Mikoyan, Anastas Ivanovich (1895–1978)*   Soviet leader. Member of the party's Politburo from 1935 to 1966. Survived successive purges and changes at the top while always remaining in a subordinate though influential position. Envoy to Budapest in 1956, where he advised against military intervention.

*Minc, Hilary (1905–74)*   Polish communist. Member of the Politbureau of the PPR, then the PZPR, from 1944 to 1956. An economic specialist, he was in charge of economic planning between 1949 and 1956. During this time he was the second most important communist in the country. Dismissed in 1956 for 'errors and distortions'.

*Moczar, Mieczysław (1913–86)*   Polish security chief and politician. Minister of Internal Affairs from 1964 to 1968. Headed the nationalist 'Partisan' faction of the PZPR in the 1960s. Made a bid for power in 1968 on an anti-Semitic and anti-intellectual platform, but was defeated at the Fifth Party Congress in November, when Gomułka refused to promote him to the Politbureau.

*Molotov, Vyacheslav Mikhailovich (1890–1986)*   Long-serving Soviet politician and associate of Stalin. In charge of foreign policy from 1939 to 1949 and 1953 to 1956. After 1953 he opposed de-Stalinization and advocated a hard line towards Eastern Europe. In 1957 he was removed from office and sent to Outer Mongolia as Soviet Ambassador.

*Nagy, Ferenc (1903–79)*   Hungarian democratic politician. Leader of the Independent Smallholders' Party from 1930 to 1947. Prime Minister of Hungary from February 1946 to May 1947. Forced out of office and out of the country in 1947. Took an active part in Hungarian exile politics in the USA.

*Nagy, Imre (1896–1958)*   Hungarian communist leader. Active in the party from the late 1920s. Spent many years in exile in the Soviet Union. Returned in 1944, becoming successively Minister of Agriculture and Minister of the Interior, until removed from office in February 1946 for insufficient ruthlessness. He remained in the party leadership but was finally expelled in 1949 for 'opportunism in agrarian matters', in other words opposition to the collectivization of agriculture. In July 1953 he was made Prime Minister on Soviet insistence, but dismissed in April 1955 after the fall of Malenkov. He returned to head the revolutionary government formed at the end of October 1956. After the defeat of the Hungarian revolution he was imprisoned by Soviet forces, tried and executed for 'conspiracy to overthrow the Hungarian People's Republic'.

*Novotný, Antonín (1904–75)*   Czech communist leader. First Secretary of the CPCz from September 1953 to January 1968, and President of Czechoslovakia from November 1957 to March 1968. Associated with Stalinism, although in the mid-1960s he permitted a degree of moderate reform. Removed from office in January 1968 by a coalition of Slovaks and economic and political reformers on the CC.

*Pauker, Ana (1893–1960)*   Romanian communist leader. Joined the RCP in 1920. In prison between 1936 and 1941. After 1945 she occupied various top party posts and was in charge of foreign affairs from 1947 to 1951. Purged in 1952 and put under house arrest for some years.

*Pavelić, Ante (1889–1959)*   Croat nationalist politician. Proclaimed Croat independence in April 1941 after the Nazi invasion of Yugoslavia. Ruled Croatia as a German satellite state from 1941 to 1945, during which time his supporters carried out massacres of Serbs and Jews. Sought as a war criminal after 1945 by the postwar Yugoslav government but escaped to the USA, where he remained.

*Radkiewicz, Stanisław (1903–87)*   Polish communist leader. Minister of Public Security between 1945 and 1954. Demoted in 1954 to the position of Minister for State Farms. Expelled from the party in 1957. Reinstated in 1960 and held various minor posts until his retirement in 1968.

*Rajk, László (1909–49)*   Hungarian communist. Joined the party in 1931. In prison from 1941 to 1944. Active in the communist underground resistance. Minister of the Interior from 1946 to 1948, Foreign Minister from 1948 to 1949. Arrested in 1949 and confessed to acting as an 'agent of imperialism'. Condemned to death and executed. Rehabilitated and reburied on 6 October 1956.

*Rákosi, Mátyás (1892–1971)*   One of the founders of the Hungarian Communist Party. In prison between 1925 and 1940, and in exile in the Soviet Union between 1940 and 1945. After his return, led the party and in effect exercised a personal dictatorship from 1948 until 1953. A fanatical and ruthless Stalinist. Dismissed in 1956.

*Révai, József (1898–1959)*   Hungarian communist intellectual. Veteran of the first Hungarian Soviet republic of 1919. In exile after that until his return to Hungary in 1945. Member of the party Politbureau from 1945 to 1953. Cultural dictator of Hungary between 1949 and 1953 in the capacity of Minister of Propaganda. Removed from office in 1953.

*Rokossowski, Marshal Konstantin (1896–1968)*   Soviet military man of Polish origin. Sent by Stalin to Poland to run the Polish army in 1949. Minister of Defence from 1949 to 1956, member of the PZPR Politbureau from 1950 to 1956. A personal symbol of Soviet domination over Poland. Recalled to the Soviet Union in 1956, where he remained subsequently.

*Šik, Ota (1919– )*   Czechoslovak economic reformer of the 1960s. Considered that economic reform had to be linked to political democratization. Deputy Prime Minister from April to August 1968. Went into exile after the Warsaw Pact invasion of August 1968.

*Slánský, Rudolf (1901–52)*   Czech communist leader. Member of the CPCz Politbureau from 1929. General Secretary of the CPCz from 1945 to 1951 and head of the state security service. Arrested in 1951 and executed in 1952 after a show trial. Posthumously rehabilitated in 1968.

*Svoboda, General Ludvík (1895–1979)*    Czech soldier. Served on the Soviet side in the Second World War. Minister of Defence from 1945 to 1950. Close to the CPCz, although not a member. Elected President of Czechoslovakia in March 1968. Refused to accept the government chosen by the Soviet leaders in August 1968. Stayed on as President after Dubček's removal in April 1969. Retired in 1975.

*Tito, Josip Broz (1892–1980)*    Founder member of the Yugoslav Communist Party. Party leader from 1937. Leader of the partisan resistance movement after 1941. Prime Minister of Yugoslavia from 1945 to 1953. President of Yugoslavia from 1953 until his death. Broke with Stalin in 1948. Introduced a system of workers' self-management after 1950, but always retained tight control of political life in the country.

*Ulbricht, Walter (1893–1973)*    German communist leader, active in the communist party throughout its legal existence. In exile in the Soviet Union during the Second World War. General Secretary of the SED from 1950 to 1971. Chairman of the Council of State from 1960 to 1973. Ruler of the GDR from its inception in 1949 until his removal from office in 1971.

*Zhivkov, Todor Khristov (1911–98)*    Bulgarian communist leader. Joined the party in 1931. Active in partisan work during the Second World War. Organized the coup of September 1944. First Secretary of the party from 1954 onwards. Prime Minister between 1962 and 1971. President from 1971 until 1989.

# BIBLIOGRAPHY

Anyone wishing to delve further into this fascinating segment of European history would be well advised to start with the general, overarching works in this list [25; 32; 36; 39; 54; 55; 59] There are two documentary collections in English [1; 20].
*Note*: the place of publication is London unless otherwise indicated.
*Abbreviation*: FRUS = *Foreign Relations of the United States.*

PRINTED PRIMARY SOURCES AND MEMOIRS

1  Daniels, R.V. (ed.), *A Documentary History of Communism. Volume 2: Communism and The World*, I.B. Tauris, 1987.
2  Djilas, M., *Conversations with Stalin*, Penguin Books, 1962.
3  Djilas, M., *Rise and Fall*, Macmillan, 1985.
4  *For a Lasting Peace, For a People's Democracy*, periodical of the Cominform 1947–56.
5  *FRUS, Diplomatic Papers, 1945, vol. II, General: Political and Economic Matters*, US Government Printing Office, Washington, DC, 1967.
6  *FRUS, Diplomatic Papers, 1945, vol. V, Europe*, US Government Printing Office, Washington, DC, 1967.
7  *FRUS, 1946, vol. VI, Eastern Europe; The Soviet Union*, US Government Printing Office, Washington, DC, 1969.
8  *FRUS, 1947, vol. IV, Eastern Europe; The Soviet Union*, US Government Printing Office, Washington, DC, 1972.
9  *FRUS, 1949, vol. V, Eastern Europe; The Soviet Union*, US Government Printing Office, Washington, DC, 1976.
10  Khrushchev, N.S., *Khrushchev Remembers*, Andre Deutsch, 1971.
11  Khrushchev, N.S., *Khrushchev Remembers. The Last Testament*, Andre Deutsch, 1974.
12  Leonhard, W., *Child of the Revolution*, Ink Links, 1979.
13  Mlynář, Z., *Night Frost in Prague: The End of Humane Socialism*, C. Hurst and Co., 1980.
14  Nagy, I., *On Communism: In Defence of the New Course*, Thames and Hudson, 1957.
15  Oxley, A., A. Pravda and A. Ritchie (eds), *Czechoslovakia, the Party and the People*, Allen Lane, 1973.
16  Polonsky, A. and B. Drukier (eds), *The Beginnings of Communist Rule in Poland, December 1943–June 1945*, Routledge and Kegan Paul, 1980.
17  Procacci, G. (ed.), *The Cominform*, Feltrinelli, Milan, 1994.
18  Remington, R.A. (ed.), *Winter in Prague*, MIT Press, Cambridge, MA, 1969.
19  *Sovetskii Soiuz i Vengerskii Krizis 1956 Goda. Dokumenty*, Rossiiskaia Politicheskaia Entsiklopediia, Moscow, 1998.

20  Stokes, G. (ed.), *From Stalinism to Pluralism: A Documentary History of Eastern Europe since 1945*, Oxford University Press, Oxford, 1991.

21  Toranska, T., *Oni: Stalin's Polish Puppets*, Collins Harvill, 1987.

22  *Vostochnaia Evropa v dokumentakh rossiiskikh arkhivov 1944–1953. Tom I, 1944–1948*, Institut Slavianovedeniia i Balkanistiki RAN, Sibirskii Khronograf, Moscow, 1997.

23  Zinner, P. (ed.), *National Communism and Popular Revolt in Eastern Europe: A Selection of Documents*, Columbia University Press, New York, 1956.


SECONDARY SOURCES: GENERAL WORKS, POLITICAL

24  Ash, T.G., *The Uses of Adversity*, Granta, 1989.

25  Berend, I.T., *Central and Eastern Europe, 1944–1993. Detour from the Periphery to the Periphery*, Cambridge University Press, Cambridge, 1996.

26  Betts, R.R. (ed.), *Central and South East Europe*, Royal Institute of International Affairs, 1950.

27  Borkenau, F., *World Communism*, University of Michigan Press, Ann Arbor, MI, 1971.

28  Brus, W., 'Stalinism and the "People's Democracies"', in R.C. Tucker (ed.), *Stalinism – Essays in Historical Interpretation*, Norton, New York, 1977.

29  Brzezinski, Z., *The Soviet Bloc. Unity and Conflict*, 2nd edn, Harvard University Press, Cambridge, MA, 1971.

30  Claudin, F., *The Communist Movement: From Comintern to Cominform*, Penguin, 1975.

31  Connor, W., *The National Question in Marxist–Leninist Theory and Strategy*, Princeton University Press, Princeton, NJ, 1984.

32  Crampton, R.J., *Eastern Europe in the Twentieth Century*, Routledge, 1994.

33  Feher, F. and A. Arato (eds), *Crisis and Reform in Eastern Europe*, Transaction Publishers, New Brunswick, NJ, 1991.

34  Fejtö, F., *Histoire des démocraties populaires*, Éditions du Seuil, Paris, 1952.

35  Fejtö, F., *A History of the People's Democracies: Eastern Europe since Stalin*, Pall Mall Press, 1971.

36  Fowkes, B., *The Rise and Fall of Communism in Eastern Europe*, 2nd edn, Macmillan, 1995.

37  Glückstein, Y., *Stalin's Satellites in Europe*, Allen and Unwin, 1952.

38  Hammond, T.T. (ed.), *The Anatomy of Communist Takeovers*, Yale University Press, New Haven, CT, 1975.

39  Held, J. (ed.), *The Columbia History of Eastern Europe in the Twentieth Century*, Columbia University Press, New York, 1992.

40  Janos, A., 'Continuity and Change in Eastern Europe: Strategies of Post-Communist Politics', in B. Crawford (ed.), *Markets, States, and Democracy. The Political Economy of Post-Communist Transformation*, Westview Press, Boulder, CO, 1995.

41  King, R.R., *Minorities under Communism. Nationalities as a Source of Tension among Balkan Communist States*, Harvard University Press, Cambridge, MA, 1973.

42  Knight, A., *Beria. Stalin's First Lieutenant*, Princeton University Press, Princeton, NJ, 1993.

43 Marcou, L., *Le Cominform*, Presses de la Fondation nationale des sciences politiques, Paris, 1977.

44 Mastny, V., *Russia's Road to the Cold War 1941–45*, Columbia University Press, New York, 1979.

45 Mastny, V., *The Cold War and Soviet Insecurity. The Stalin Years*, Oxford University Press, Oxford, 1996.

46 McCagg, W.O., *Stalin Embattled: 1943–48*, Wayne State University Press, Detroit, MI, 1978.

47 McCauley, M. (ed.), *Communist Power in Europe 1944–49*, Macmillan, 1977.

48 McCauley, M., *The Origins of the Cold War 1941–1949*, 2nd edn, Longman, 1995.

49 McDermott, K. and J. Agnew, *The Comintern. A History of International Communism from Lenin to Stalin*, Macmillan, 1996.

50 Morton, H.W. and R.L. Tőkés (eds), *Soviet Politics and Society in the 1970s*, Collier Macmillan, New York, 1974.

51 Naimark, N.M. and L. Gibianskii (eds), *The Establishment of Communist Regimes in Eastern Europe, 1944–1949*, Westview Press, Boulder, CO, 1997.

52 Resis, A., 'The Churchill–Stalin Percentage Agreement', *American Historical Review*, 83, 2 (April 1978), pp. 358–87.

53 Rothschild, J., *East Central Europe between the Two World Wars*, University of Washington Press, Seattle, WA, 1974.

54 Rothschild, J., *Return to Diversity. A Political History of East Central Europe since World War II*, 2nd edn, Oxford University Press, Oxford, 1993.

55 Rupnik, J., *The Other Europe*, Weidenfeld and Nicolson, 1988.

56 Seton-Watson, H., *The East European Revolutions*, Methuen, 1950.

57 Spriano, P., *Stalin and the European Communists*, Verso, 1985.

58 Urban, G.R. (ed.), *Communist Reformation. Nationalism, Internationalism and Change in the World Communist Movement*, Maurice Temple Smith, 1979.

59 Wolff, R.L., *The Balkans in Our Time*, Harvard University Press, Cambridge, MA, 1956.

## GENERAL WORKS, SOCIAL, ECONOMIC AND CULTURAL

60 Aldcroft, D.H., *The European Economy 1914–1990*, 3rd edn, Routledge, 1993.

61 Balawyder, A. (ed.), *Cooperative Movements in Eastern Europe*, Macmillan, 1980.

62 Batt, J., *Economic Reform and Political Change in Eastern Europe*, Macmillan, 1988.

63 Brus, W., 'The East European Economic Reforms: What Happened to Them?', *Soviet Studies*, 21, 2 (1979), pp. 257–67.

64 Brus, W. and K. Laski, *From Marx to the Market. Socialism in Search of an Economic System*, Clarendon Press, Oxford, 1989.

65 Carlton, R.K. (ed.), *Forced Labour in the 'People's Democracies'*, Mid-European Studies Center, Inc., New York, 1955.

66 Chirot, D. (ed.), *The Origins of Backwardness in Eastern Europe*, University of California Press, Berkeley, CA, 1989.

67 Connor, W.D., *Socialism, Politics and Equality*, Columbia University Press, New York, 1979.

68  Djilas, M., *The New Class: An Analysis of the Communist System*, Harcourt, Brace and Company, San Diego, CA, 1985.
69  Eberstadt, N., 'Health and Mortality in Eastern Europe, 1965–85', *Communist Economies*, 2, 3 (1990), pp. 347–71.
70  *Economic Survey of Europe in 1956*, United Nations, New York, 1957.
71  *Economic Survey of Europe in 1969, Part I: Structural Trends and Prospects in the European Economy*, United Nations, New York, 1970.
72  Gati, C. (ed.), *The Politics of Modernization in Eastern Europe*, Praeger Publishers, New York, 1974.
73  Grossman, G., 'Economic Reforms in Eastern Europe. A Balance Sheet', *Problems of Communism*, November–December 1966, pp. 43–55.
74  Heitlinger, A., *Women and State Socialism*, Macmillan, 1979.
75  Jancar, B., *Women under Communism*, Johns Hopkins University Press, Baltimore, MD, 1978.
76  Jowitt, K., 'Inclusion and Mobilization in European Leninist Regimes', *World Politics*, vol. 28, no. 1, October 1975, pp. 69–96.
77  Kaplan, K., *The Council for Mutual Economic Aid, 1949–1951*, Research Project 'Experiences of the Prague Spring', no. 4, Index, Cologne, 1979.
78  Kaser, M., *Comecon. Integration Problems of the Planned Economies*, 2nd edn, Oxford University Press, Oxford, 1967.
79  Kaser, M.C. and E.A. Radice (eds), *The Economic History of Eastern Europe 1919–1975*, vol. 1, Clarendon Press, Oxford, 1985.
80  Kaser, M.C. and E.A. Radice (eds), *The Economic History of Eastern Europe 1919–1975*, vol. 2, Clarendon Press, Oxford, 1986.
81  Kaser, M.C. (ed.), *The Economic History of Eastern Europe 1919–1975*, vol. 3, Clarendon Press, Oxford, 1986.
82  Kende, P. and Z. Strzemiska, *Equality and Inequality in Eastern Europe*, Berg Publishers Ltd., Leamington Spa, 1987.
83  Kornai, J., *The Socialist System. The Political Economy of Communism*, Clarendon Press, Oxford, 1992.
84  Matejko, A., *Social Change and Stratification in Eastern Europe*, Pall Mall Press, 1974.
85  McIntyre, R.J., 'Pronatalist Programmes in Eastern Europe', *Soviet Studies*, 27, 3 (July 1975), pp. 366–80.
86  Metcalf, L.K., *The CMEA. The Failure of Reform*, Columbia University Press, New York, 1997.
87  Millar, J.R. and S.L. Wolchik (eds), *The Social Legacy of Communism*, Cambridge University Press, Cambridge, 1994.
88  Nove, A., H.-H. Höhmann and G. Seidenstecher (eds), *The East European Economies in the 1970s*, Butterworths, 1982.
89  Porket, J.L., 'Czech Women under Soviet-Type Socialism', *Slavonic and East European Review*, 59 (1981), pp. 241–63.
90  Potts, M., 'Legal Abortion in Eastern Europe', *The Eugenics Review*, 59, 4 (1967), pp. 232–50.
91  Ramet, P. (ed.), *Religion and Nationalism in Soviet and East European Politics*, Duke University Press, Durham, NC, 1989.
92  Sampson, S., 'The Second Economy', *Annals of the American Association*, 493 (1986), pp. 120–36.

93   Smith, A.H., *The Planned Economies of Eastern Europe*, Croom Helm, 1983.
94   Spulber, N., *The Economics of Communist Eastern Europe*, MIT Press, Cambridge, MA, 1957.
95   Todorova, M., *Imagining the Balkans*, Oxford University Press, Oxford, 1997.
96   Tőkés, R.L. (ed.), *Opposition in Eastern Europe*, Macmillan, 1979.
97   Van Brabant, J.M., *Socialist Economic Integration*, Cambridge University Press, Cambridge, 1980.
98   Wädekin, K.-E., *Sozialistische Agrarpolitik in Osteuropa*, vol. 1, Duncker and Humblot, Berlin, 1974.
99   Wiles, P., *Communist International Economics*, Oxford University Press, Oxford, 1969.
100  Winiecki, J., 'Are Soviet-Type Economies Entering an Era of Long-term Decline?', *Soviet Studies*, 38, 3 (July 1986), pp. 325–48.
101  Winiecki, J., *The Distorted World of Soviet-Type Economies*, Routledge, 1988.
102  Wolchik, S. and A.G. Meyer (eds), *Women, State and Party in Eastern Europe*, Duke University Press, Durham, NC, 1985.
103  Zwass, A., *The Economies of Eastern Europe in a Time of Change*, Macmillan, 1984.

## SECONDARY SOURCES: COUNTRY BY COUNTRY LIST

### *Bulgaria*

104  Bell, J.D., *The Communist Party of Bulgaria from Blagoev to Zhivkov*, Hoover Institution Press, Stanford, CA, 1986.
105  Boll, M.M., *Cold War in the Balkans. American Foreign Policy and the Emergence of Communist Bulgaria 1943–1947*, University of Kentucky Press, Lexington, KY, 1984.
106  Brown, J.F., *Bulgaria under Communist Rule*, Pall Mall Press, 1970.
107  Crampton, R.J., *A Concise History of Bulgaria*, Cambridge University Press, Cambridge, 1997.
108  Lampe, J.R., *The Bulgarian Economy in the Twentieth Century*, Croom Helm, 1986.
109  Markov, G., *The Truth that Killed*, Weidenfeld and Nicolson, 1983.
110  Migev, Vl., 'The Bulgarian Peasants' Resistance to Collectivization, 1948–1958', *Bulgarian Historical Review/Revue bulgare de l'histoire*, 25, 1 (1997), pp. 53–71.
111  Miller, M.L., *Bulgaria during the Second World War*, Stanford University Press, Stanford, CA, 1975.
112  Oren, N., *Bulgarian Communism: The Road to Power 1934–1944*, Columbia University Press, New York, 1971.
113  Oren, N., *Revolution Administered: Agrarianism and Communism in Bulgaria*, Johns Hopkins University Press, Baltimore, MD, 1973.

## Czechoslovakia

114   Bloomfield, J., *Passive Revolution: Politics and the Czechoslovak Working Class*, Allison and Busby, 1979.
115   Connelly, J., 'Students, Workers and Social Change: The Limits of Czech Stalinism', *Slavic Review*, 56, 2 (summer 1997), pp. 307–35.
116   Fejtö, F., *Le Coup de Prague 1948*, Éditions du Seuil, Paris, 1976.
117   Golan, G., *The Czechoslovak Reform Movement: Communism in Crisis, 1962–1968*, Cambridge University Press, Cambridge, 1971.
118   Hejzlar, Z., *Reformkommunismus. Zur Geschichte der Kommunistischen Partei der Tschechoslowakei*, Europäische Verlagsanstalt, Cologne, 1976.
119   Kaplan, K., *Dans les archives du Comité Central*, Éditions Albin Michel, Paris, 1978.
120   Kaplan, K., *Das verhängnisvolle Bündnis. Unterwanderung, Gleichschaltung und Vernichtung der tschechoslowakischen Sozialdemokratie 1944–1954*, Pol-Verlag, Wuppertal, 1984.
121   Kaplan, K., *Die Politischen Prozesse in der Tschechoslowakei 1948–54*, Oldenbourg Verlag, Munich, 1986.
122   Kaplan, K., *The Overcoming of the Regime Crisis after Stalin's Death in Czechoslovakia, Poland and Hungary*, Index, Cologne, 1986.
123   Kaplan, K., *The Short March: The Communist Takeover in Czechoslovakia*, Hurst, 1987.
124   Kaplan, K., 'Tabory nucené Prace v Československu v letech 1948–1954', *Sešity Ustavu pro soudobé dějiny ČSAV*, vol. 3, Ústav pro soudobé dějiny ČSAV, Prague, 1992.
125   Kosta, J., *Abriss der sozialökokomischen Entwicklung der Tschechoslowakei 1945–1977*, Suhrkamp Verlag, Frankfurt am Main, 1978.
126   Kovanda, K., 'Works Councils in Czechoslovakia 1945–1947', *Soviet Studies*, 29, 2 (April 1977), pp. 255–69.
127   Krejči, J. and P. Machonin, *Czechoslovakia, 1918–92. A Laboratory for Social Change*, Macmillan, 1996.
128   Murashko, G.P., 'Fevral'ski Krizis 1948 g. v Chekhoslovakii i Sovetskoe Rukovodstvo', *Novaia i Noveishaia Istoriia*, 3 (1998), pp. 50–63.
129   Šimečka, M., *The Restoration of Order. The Normalization of Czechoslovakia*, Verso, 1984.
130   Skilling, G., 'Revolution and Continuity in Czechoslovakia 1945–46', *Journal of Central European Affairs*, 20, 4 (January 1961), pp. 357–77.
131   Skilling, G., *Czechoslovakia's Interrupted Revolution*, Princeton University Press, Princeton, NJ, 1976.
132   Williams, K., *The Prague Spring and its Aftermath. Czechoslovak Politics, 1968–1970*, Cambridge University Press, Cambridge, 1997.
133   Zinner, P.E., *Communist Strategy and Tactics in Czechoslovakia, 1918–48*, Pall Mall Press, 1963.

## East Germany

134   Fulbrook, Mary, *Anatomy of Dictatorship. Inside the GDR, 1949–1989*, Oxford University Press, Oxford, 1995.

135 Kopstein, J., *The Politics of Economic Decline in East Germany, 1945–1989*, University of North Carolina Press, Chapel Hill, NC, 1997.

136 Krisch, H., *German Politics under Soviet Occupation*, Columbia University Press, New York, 1974.

137 McCauley, M., *The German Democratic Republic since 1945*, Macmillan, 1983.

138 Naimark, N.H., *The Russians in Germany. A History of the Soviet Zone of Occupation, 1945–1949*, Harvard University Press, Cambridge, MA, 1995.

139 Sandford, G.W., *From Hitler to Ulbricht: The Communist Reconstruction of East Germany 1945–1946*, Princeton University Press, Princeton, NJ, 1983.

140 Staritz, D., *Sozialismus in einem halben Land*, Verlag Klaus Wagenbach, Berlin, 1978.

140a Staritz, D., *Geschichte der DDR 1949–1985*, Suhrkamp Verlag, Frankfurt am Main, 1985.

141 Steininger, R., *Deutsche Geschichte seit 1945. Darstellung und Dokumente in vier Bänden, Band 2: 1948–1955*, Fischer Taschenbuch Verlag, Frankfurt am Main, 1996.


*Hungary*

142 Aczél, T. and T. Méray, *The Revolt of the Mind*, Thames and Hudson, 1960.

143 Balassa, B.A., *The Hungarian Experience in Economic Planning*, Yale University Press, New Haven, CT, 1959.

144 Fehér, F. and A. Heller, *Hungary 1956 Revisited*, Allen and Unwin, 1983.

145 Gati, C., *Hungary and the Soviet Bloc*, Duke University Press, Durham, NC, 1986.

146 Hankiss, E., *East European Alternatives*, Oxford University Press, Oxford, 1990.

147 Hoensch, J.K., *A History of Modern Hungary 1867–1994*, 2nd edn, Longman, 1996.

148 Ignotus, Paul, *Hungary*, Ernest Benn Ltd., 1972.

149 Kornai, J., 'The Hungarian Reform Process', in F. Fehér and A. Arato (eds), *Crisis and Reform in Eastern Europe*, Transaction Publishers, New Brunswick, NJ, 1991, pp. 27–98.

150 Kovrig, B., *Communism in Hungary: From Kun to Kádár*, Hoover Institution Press, Stanford, CA, 1979.

151 Litván, G. (ed.), *The Hungarian Revolution of 1956: Reform, Revolt and Repression*, Longman, 1996.

152 Lomax, B., *Hungary 1956*, Allison and Busby, 1976.

153 Molnár, M., *From Béla Kun to János Kádár: Seventy Years of Hungarian Communism*, Berg Publishers, Oxford, 1990.

154 Musatov, V.L., 'SSSR i Vengerskie Sobytiia 1956 g.: Novye arkhivnye Materialy', *Novaia i Noveishaia Istoriia*, 1 (1993), pp. 3–22.

155 Váli, F.A., *Rift and Revolt in Hungary*, Harvard University Press, Cambridge, MA, 1961.

## Poland

156   Coutividis, J. and J. Reynolds, *Poland 1939–1947*, Leicester University Press, Leicester, 1986.
157   Davies, N., *God's Playground. A History of Poland*, vol. 2, Oxford University Press, Oxford, 1981.
158   Drewnowski, J., 'The Central Planning Office on Trial. The Beginnings of Stalinism in Poland', *Soviet Studies*, 31, 1 (1979), pp. 23–42.
159   Dziewanowski, M.K., *The Communist Party of Poland*, 2nd edn, Harvard University Press, Cambridge, MA, 1977.
160   Halecki, O. (ed.), *Poland*, Atlantic Books, 1957.
161   Hiscocks, R., *Poland: Bridge for the Abyss?*, Oxford University Press, Oxford, 1963.
162   Kennedy, P., *Rebuilding Poland. Workers and Communists 1945–1950*, Cornell University Press, Ithaca, NY, 1997.
163   Kenney, P., 'Remaking the Polish Working Class: Early Stalinist Models of Labor and Leisure', *Slavic Review*, 53, 1 (spring 1994), pp. 1–25.
164   Kersten, K., *The Establishment of Communist Rule in Poland 1943–1948*, University of California Press, Berkeley, CA, 1991.
165   Korbonski, A., *The Politics of Socialist Agriculture in Poland 1945–60*, Columbia University Press, New York, 1965.
166   Lane, D. and G. Kolankiewicz (eds), *Social Groups in Polish Society*, Macmillan, 1973.
167   Leslie, R.F. (ed.), *The History of Poland since 1863*, Cambridge University Press, Cambridge, 1983.
168   Milosz, C., *The History of Polish Literature*, Macmillan, 1969.
169   Montias, J.H., *Central Planning in Poland*, New Haven, CT, 1962.
170   Monticone, R.C., *The Catholic Church in Communist Poland 1945–1985. Forty Years of Church–State Relations*, Columbia University Press, New York, 1986.
171   Reynolds, J., 'Communists, Socialists and Workers. Poland 1944–48', *Soviet Studies*, 30, 4 (October 1978), pp. 516–39.
172   Stehle, H.-J., *The Independent Satellite: Society and Politics in Poland since 1945*, Praeger, New York, 1965.
173   Syrop, K., *Spring in October*, Weidenfeld and Nicolson, 1957.

## Romania

174   Deletant, D., 'Soviet Influence in the Romanian Security Apparatus 1944–1953, *Revue Roumaine d'Histoire*, 33, 3–4 (July–December 1994), pp. 345–53.
175   Ionescu, G., *Communism in Rumania, 1944–1962*, Oxford University Press, Oxford, 1964.
176   Jowitt, K., *Revolutionary Breakthroughs and National Development: The Case of Romania, 1944–1965*, University of California Press, Berkeley, CA, 1971.
177   King, R.R., *A History of the Romanian Communist Party*, Hoover Institution Press, Stanford, CA, 1980.

178 Roberts, H.L., *Rumania: Political Problems of an Agrarian State*, Yale University Press, New Haven, CT, 1951.
179 Shafir, M., *Romania. Politics, Economics and Society. Political Stagnation and Simulated Change*, Frances Pinter, 1985.


## Yugoslavia and Albania

180 Banac, I., *With Stalin Against Tito. Cominformist Splits in Yugoslav Communism*, Cornell University Press, Ithaca, NY, 1988.
181 Cohen, L.J., *Broken Bonds. Yugoslavia's Disintegration. Balkan Politics in Transition*, 2nd edn, Westview Press, Boulder, CO, 1995.
182 Denitch, B., *The Legitimation of a Revolution. The Yugoslav Case*, Yale University Press, New Haven, CT, 1976.
183 Djilas, A., *The Contested Country. Yugoslav Unity and Communist Revolution 1919–1953*, Harvard University Press, Cambridge, MA, 1991.
184 Gregory, M.B., 'Regional Economic Development in Yugoslavia', *Soviet Studies*, 25, 2 (October 1973), pp. 213–28.
185 Hoffman, G.W. and F.W. Neal, *Yugoslavia and the New Communism*, Twentieth Century Fund, New York, 1962.
186 Johnson, A.R., 'Yugoslavia and the Sino-Soviet Conflict: The Shifting Triangle, 1948–1974', *Studies in Comparative Communism*, 7, 1 and 2 (1974), pp. 184–203.
187 Koštunica, V. and K. Čavoški, *Party Pluralism and Monism. Social Movements and the Political System in Yugoslavia 1944–49*, Columbia University Press, New York, 1985.
188 Lampe, J., *Yugoslavia as History. Twice There was a Country*, Cambridge University Press, Cambridge, 1996.
189 Logoreci, A., *The Albanians: Europe's Forgotten Survivors*, Gollancz, 1971.
190 Malcolm, N., *Bosnia – A Short History*, Macmillan, 1994.
191 Ramet, P., *Nationalism and Federalism in Yugoslavia, 1963–1983*, Indiana University Press, Bloomington, IN, 1984.
192 Rusinow, D., *The Yugoslav Experiment 1948–74*, C. Hurst and Co., 1977.
193 Shoup, P., *Communism and the Yugoslav National Question*, Columbia University Press, New York, 1968.
194 Singleton, F., *Twentieth Century Yugoslavia*, Macmillan, 1979.
195 Wilson, D., *Tito's Yugoslavia*, Cambridge University Press, Cambridge, 1979.

# SEMINAR STUDIES | IN HISTORY

General Editors:   Clive Emsley & Gordon Martel

The series was founded by Patrick Richardson in 1966. Between 1980 and 1996 Roger Lockyer edited the series before handing over to Clive Emsley (Professor of History at the Open University) and Gordon Martel (Professor of International History at the University of Northern British Columbia, Canada and Senior Research Fellow at De Montfort University).

## MEDIEVAL ENGLAND

The Pre-Reformation Church in England 1400–1530 (Second edition)
*Christopher Harper-Bill*                                          0 582 28989 0

Lancastrians and Yorkists: The Wars of the Roses
*David R Cook*                                                    0 582 35384 X

## TUDOR ENGLAND

Henry VII (Third edition)
*Roger Lockyer & Andrew Thrush*                                   0 582 20912 9

Henry VIII (Second edition)
*M D Palmer*                                                      0 582 35437 4

Tudor Rebellions (Fourth edition)
*Anthony Fletcher & Diarmaid MacCulloch*                          0 582 28990 4

The Reign of Mary I (Second edition)
*Robert Tittler*                                                  0 582 06107 5

Early Tudor Parliaments 1485–1558
*Michael A R Graves*                                              0 582 03497 3

The English Reformation 1530–1570
*W J Sheils*                                                      0 582 35398 X

Elizabethan Parliaments 1559–1601 (Second edition)
*Michael A R Graves*                                              0 582 29196 8

England and Europe 1485–1603 (Second edition)
*Susan Doran*                                                     0 582 28991 2

The Church of England 1570–1640
*Andrew Foster*                                                   0 582 35574 5

## STUART BRITAIN

Social Change and Continuity: England 1550–1750 (Second edition)
*Barry Coward*                                                    0 582 29442 8

James I (Second edition)
*S J Houston*                                                     0 582 20911 0

The English Civil War 1640–1649
*Martyn Bennett*                                                 0 582 35392 0

Charles I, 1625–1640
*Brian Quintrell*                                                0 582 00354 7

The English Republic 1649–1660 (Second edition)
*Toby Barnard*                                                   0 582 08003 7

Radical Puritans in England 1550–1660
*R J Acheson*                                                     0 582 35515 X

The Restoration and the England of Charles II (Second edition)
*John Miller*                                                    0 582 29223 9

The Glorious Revolution (Second edition)
*John Miller*                                                    0 582 29222 0

## EARLY MODERN EUROPE

The Renaissance (Second edition)
*Alison Brown*                                                   0 582 30781 3

The Emperor Charles V
*Martyn Rady*                                                    0 582 35475 7

French Renaissance Monarchy: Francis I and Henry II (Second edition)
*Robert Knecht*                                                  0 582 28707 3

The Protestant Reformation in Europe
*Andrew Johnston*                                                0 582 07020 1

The French Wars of Religion 1559–1598 (Second edition)
*Robert Knecht*                                                  0 582 28533 X

Phillip II
*Geoffrey Woodward*                                              0 582 07232 8

The Thirty Years' War
*Peter Limm*                                                     0 582 35373 4

Louis XIV
*Peter Campbell*                                                 0 582 01770 X

Spain in the Seventeenth Century
*Graham Darby*                                                   0 582 07234 4

Peter the Great
*William Marshall*                                               0 582 00355 5

## EUROPE 1789–1918

Britain and the French Revolution
*Clive Emsley*                                                    0 582 36961 4

Revolution and Terror in France 1789–1795 (Second edition)
*D G Wright*                                                      0 582 00379 2

Napoleon and Europe
*D G Wright*                                                      0 582 35457 9

Nineteenth-Century Russia: Opposition to Autocracy
*Derek Offord*                                                   0 582 35767 5

The Constitutional Monarchy in France 1814–48
*Pamela Pilbeam*                                                  0 582 31210 8

The 1848 Revolutions (Second edition)
*Peter Jones*                                                     0 582 06106 7

The Italian Risorgimento
*M Clark*                                                         0 582 00353 9

Bismark & Germany 1862–1890 (Second edition)
*D G Williamson*                                                  0 582 29321 9

Imperial Germany 1890–1918
*Ian Porter, Ian Armour and Roger Lockyer*                        0 582 03496 5

The Dissolution of the Austro-Hungarian Empire 1867–1918 (Second edition)
*John W Mason*                                                    0 582 29466 5

Second Empire and Commune: France 1848–1871 (Second edition)
*William H C Smith*                                               0 582 28705 7

France 1870–1914 (Second edition)
*Robert Gildea*                                                   0 582 29221 2

The Scramble for Africa  (Second edition)
*M E Chamberlain*                                                 0 582 36881 2

Late Imperial Russia 1890–1917
*John F Hutchinson*                                               0 582 32721 0

The First World War
*Stuart Robson*                                                   0 582 31556 5


## EUROPE SINCE 1918

The Russian Revolution (Second edition)
*Anthony Wood*                                                    0 582 35559 1

Lenin's Revolution: Russia, 1917–1921
*David Marples*                                                   0 582 31917 X

Stalin and Stalinism (Second edition)
*Martin McCauley*                                                 0 582 27658 6

The Weimar Republic (Second edition)
*John Hiden*                                              0 582 28706 5

The Inter-War Crisis 1919–1939
*Richard Overy*                                           0 582 35379 3

Fascism and the Right in Europe, 1919–1945
*Martin Blinkhorn*                                        0 582 07021 X

Spain's Civil War (Second edition)
*Harry Browne*                                            0 582 28988 2

The Third Reich (Second edition)
*D G Williamson*                                          0 582 20914 5

The Origins of the Second World War (Second edition)
*R J Overy*                                               0 582 29085 6

The Second World War in Europe
*Paul MacKenzie*                                          0 582 32692 3

Anti-Semitism before the Holocaust
*Albert S Lindemann*                                      0 582 36964 9

The Holocaust: The Third Reich and the Jews
*David Engel*                                             0 582 32720 2

Britain and Europe since 1945
*Alex May*                                                0 582 30778 3

Eastern Europe 1945–1969: From Stalinism to Stagnation
*Ben Fowkes*                                              0 582 32693 1

The Khrushchev Era, 1953–1964
*Martin McCauley*                                         0 582 27776 0


## NINETEENTH-CENTURY BRITAIN

Britain before the Reform Acts: Politics and Society 1815–1832
*Eric J Evans*                                            0 582 00265 6

Parliamentary Reform in Britain c. 1770–1918
*Eric J Evans*                                            0 582 29467 3

Democracy and Reform 1815–1885
*D G Wright*                                              0 582 31400 3

Poverty and Poor Law Reform in Nineteenth-Century Britain, 1834–1914:
From Chadwick to Booth
*David Englander*                                         0 582 31554 9

The Birth of Industrial Britain: Economic Change, 1750–1850
*Kenneth Morgan*                                          0 582 29833 4

Chartism (Third edition)
*Edward Royle*                                            0 582 29080 5

Peel and the Conservative Party 1830–1850
*Paul Adelman*                                            0 582 35557 5

Gladstone, Disraeli and later Victorian Politics (Third edition)
*Paul Adelman* — 0 582 29322 7

Britain and Ireland: From Home Rule to Independence
*Jeremy Smith* — 0 582 30193 9

## TWENTIETH-CENTURY BRITAIN

The Rise of the Labour Party 1880–1945 (Third edition)
*Paul Adelman* — 0 582 29210 7

The Conservative Party and British Politics 1902–1951
*Stuart Ball* — 0 582 08002 9

The Decline of the Liberal Party 1910–1931 (Second edition)
*Paul Adelman* — 0 582 27733 7

The British Women's Suffrage Campaign 1866–1928
*Harold L Smith* — 0 582 29811 3

War & Society in Britain 1899–1948
*Rex Pope* — 0 582 03531 7

The British Economy since 1914: A Study in Decline?
*Rex Pope* — 0 582 30194 7

Unemployment in Britain between the Wars
*Stephen Constantine* — 0 582 35232 0

The Attlee Governments 1945–1951
*Kevin Jefferys* — 0 582 06105 9

The Conservative Governments 1951–1964
*Andrew Boxer* — 0 582 20913 7

Britain under Thatcher
*Anthony Seldon and Daniel Collings* — 0 582 31714 2

## INTERNATIONAL HISTORY

The Eastern Question 1774–1923 (Second edition)
*A L Macfie* — 0 582 29195 X

The Origins of the First World War (Second edition)
*Gordon Martel* — 0 582 28697 2

The United States and the First World War
*Jennifer D Keene* — 0 582 35620 2

Anti-Semitism before the Holocaust
*Albert S Lindemann* — 0 582 36964 9

The Origins of the Cold War, 1941–1949 (Second edition)
*Martin McCauley* — 0 582 27659 4

Russia, America and the Cold War, 1949–1991
*Martin McCauley* — 0 582 27936 4

The Arab–Israeli Conflict
*Kirsten E Schulze*                                                    0 582 31646 4

The United Nations since 1945: Peacekeeping and the Cold War
*Norrie MacQueen*                                                     0 582 35673 3

Decolonisation: The British Experience since 1945
*Nicholas J White*                                                   0 582 29087 2

The Vietnam War
*Mitchell Hall*                                                      0 582 32859 4


## WORLD HISTORY

China in Transformation 1900–1949
*Colin Mackerras*                                                    0 582 31209 4


## US HISTORY

America in the Progressive Era, 1890–1914
*Lewis L Gould*                                                      0 582 35671 7

The United States and the First World War
*Jennifer D Keene*                                                   0 582 35620 2

The Truman Years, 1945–1953
*Mark S Byrnes*                                                      0 582 32904 3

The Vietnam War
*Mitchell Hall*                                                      0 582 32859 4